The Naturalists Library V27: Monkeys

William Jardine

THE

NATURALIST'S LIBRARY.

EDITED BY

SIR WILLIAM JARDINE, BART.

F.R.S.E., F.L.S., ETC. ETC.

VOL. XXVII.

𝔐ammalia.

MONKEYS.

BY THE EDITOR.

𝔏onbon:

CHATTO & WINDUS, PICCADILLY.

THE
NATURALIST'S LIBRARY.

MAMMALIA.

Stewart delt.   Lizars sc.

Rhesus Monkey.
Young.

LONDON, CHATTO & WINDUS
PICCADILLY

BUFFON

Le Cte de Buffon

Engraved for the Naturalists Library

CONTENTS.

CONTENTS.

CONTENTS.

CONTENTS.

CONTENTS.

MEMOIR OF BUFFON.

B

MEMOIR OF BUFFON.

It is a remarkable circumstance, that among the many naturalists whose names at this period are remembered from the high reputation of their works, comparatively few, had their minds early directed by their parents or guardians to the study of this science, and by many, it was not commenced before a somewhat advanced age. The illustrious naturalist whom we have chosen for the subject of the present memoir, is an instance among many others; and although he was fortunate in procuring an education of the most liberal kind, which embraced in its range polite literature and the sciences, and was extended by means of foreign travel and the companionship of polished minds, he had passed his thirtieth year before designing the plan of his extensive works on nature, and the first branches of the animal kingdom.

George Louis le Clerc Buffon was born at Montbard* in Burgundy, in September 1707, and his father,

* Buffon's house seemed the large habitation of a tradesman rather than the residence of a man of rank. It is in the High

Benjamin le Clerc Buffon, being a counsellor of Parliament in the district, naturally wished that his son should study his own profession, and if possible assist and succeed him in the discharge of its duties. There are few existing records of the early life of Buffon; and except that he pursued the studies which he undertook with great ardour and perseverance, we know little of his youthful habits and propensities.

His first public tuition was at the Jesuit's College of Dijon, where he was placed to study the profession of the law; but his dislike for this employment, and the zeal with which he followed the more abstruse sciences, prevented his father from insisting upon a continuation of his legal studies, and gradually permitted him to pursue those of his own selecting. Astronomy and mathematics seem to have been the branches which chiefly interested him; and he perused, with perseverance, the most esteemed works on these subjects. Euclid was a great favourite; and he is said to have been so much engrossed with this author, that he

Street, and the court is behind. You ascend a staircase to go into the garden, which is raised on the ruins of the ancient mansion, of which the walls make the terraces. On the top there still remains an octagon tower, where Buffon made his observations on the reverberations of air. The elevation of this tower is 140 feet above the level of the little river Braine, which crosses the town. This singular and picturesque garden is well worthy the notice of the curious; and the numerous foreign trees which the illustrious proprietor had collected, form agreeable arbours.—MILLIN's *Travels*.

always carried a copy in his pocket, and was often observed to retire from his companions at play, and to attempt, in some solitary corner, the resolution of any problem with which he had been perplexed.

This constant study and perseverance, at a period so early, and when youthful minds are generally most idly inclined, was attended with very brilliant results. He is even said to have anticipated Newton in some of his most remarkable discoveries, and in after life withheld the circumstances, upon a principle of some singularity, and at variance with his failing of vanity: he said, " that nobody was obliged to believe it."

At the college of Dijon he became acquainted with Lord Kingston, a young nobleman who was travelling, accompanied by a tutor. Buffon fortunately became acquainted with both; and the latter, being a man of considerable attainments, and devoted to the sciences, found a ready access to the mind of a youth endowed with such temper and abilities. It was agreed that he should accompany them in the prosecution of their travels, and he became equally acceptable to his friends, and pleased with their society; afterwards remarking, that while the one became his companion in pleasure and amusements, the other gained his esteem by his more solid qualifications.

They travelled onwards to Italy; and here, amidst all that is placid and sublime in nature, or lovely in the arts, he continued to pursue the more abstracted departments of science, almost neglecting the artificial productions; and at this same period seems to have imbibed many of the theories and ideas, which fancifully, but eloquently, adorn the chapters of the first volumes of his great work.

During the period of these travels Buffon lost his mother;* and by her death, before he had attained his majority, succeeded to an income of nearly twelve thousand pounds yearly. An accession of such amount to his fortune, enabled him to follow out every design which his studies had suggested; but it also allowed him to pursue, with almost unlimited control, every indulgence which his inclinations prompted. His European travels still appear to have been continued, and after his return to Montbard, being embroiled in some affair of honour which required his absence until matters were arranged, he visited Paris and England, and did not finally settle at his paternal residence, till about the age of twenty-five, when he determined quietly to pursue the studies in which he had so much delighted. He seems to have laid down for himself, even at this early period, a decided and rigorous division of his time, and to have attended generally to the Sciences, Natural History, and Polite Literature.

The division of his time and labour is thus detailed by a modern biographer: " After he was dressed, he dictated letters, and regulated his domestic affairs;

---

* The maiden name of his mother was Mademoiselle de Merlin.

and at six o'clock he regulated his studies at the pavilion called the Tower of St Louis.   This pavilion was
situated at the extremity of the garden, about a fur-
long from the house ; and the only furniture which it
contained was a large wooden secretary and an arm-
chair.   No books or pictures relieved the naked appearance of the apartment, or distracted the thoughts
of the learned possessor.   The entrance was by green
folding-doors, the walls were painted green, and the
interior had the appearance of a chapel, on account of
the elevation of the roof.   Within this was another
cabinet, where Buffon resided the greater part of the
year, on account of the coldness of the other apartment, and where he composed the greater number of
his works.   It was a small square building, situated
on the side of a terrace, and was ornamented with
drawings of birds and beasts.   Prince Henry of Prussia
called it the cradle of natural history ; and Rousseau,
before he entered it, used to fall on his knees and kiss
the threshold.   At nine o'clock, Buffon usually took
an hour's rest ; and his breakfast, which consisted of
a piece of bread and two glasses of wine, was brought
to the pavilion.   When he had written two hours after
breakfast, he returned to the house.   At dinner he
spent a considerable portion of time, and indulged in
all the gayeties and trifles which occurred at table.
After dinner, he slept an hour in his room, took a
solitary walk, and during the rest of the evening, he
either conversed with his family or guests, or sat at

his desk examining the papers which were submitted
to his judgment. At nine o'clock he went to bed, to
prepare himself for the same routine of judgment and
pleasure. In this manner were spent no fewer than
fifty years of his life."

During the whole period of Buffon's career, we find
him particular and anxious, regarding the purity and
elegance of his style ; and he translated many standard
works in various languages with the view of improving
it. The first of these which he published, was "Hales's
Vegetable Statics," and (from the Latin) an edition
of Newton's Fluxions ; both were accompanied with
appropriate prefaces of considerable length and ability.
The latter work coincided with the turn of mind which
he exhibited in his early studies, and the first was
most likely commenced, with the double purpose of
improving his knowledge in the English language, and
of increasing his acquaintance with the extensive woods
which occupied a great part of his property, and were
of much importance in his annual revenue. At this
time he also instituted and carried through experiments, to prove the relative strength of the different
woods which were used in France for purposes of
public utility, and the best season for cutting the
timber.

The next subject with which he became interested,
was the manner in which the Roman fleet under command of Marcellus, was set on fire by Archimedes,
and which was supposed, could not be accomplished

by means of burning mirrors, as has been recorded.[*]
Buffon commenced his researches with his usual
ardour and perseverance, and his experiments were
eminently successful. They are the most important which he performed, in those branches uncon-
nected with natural history, and it is probable
that, had he not been appointed Intendant of the
Royal Garden and Cabinet, the various branches of
mathematics, optics, &c., would have received the
greatest part of his attention, and might have been
attended with the most splendid results. We consider
therefore that a short sketch of the progress of these
experiments may be interesting.

Buffon commenced his researches, with the view of
constructing a burning mirror, which would be capable of performing, what had been thought Archimedes
could not have executed ; but, before commencing the
plan, it was necessary to perform many preliminary
experiments, relating to the loss of light by reflection,
and the best materials which could be used for the con-

[*] When the fleet of Marcellus was within bow-shot, the old
man (Archimedes) brought out a hexagonal mirror which he had
made : he placed at proper distances from this mirror other smaller
mirrors, which were of the same kind, and which were moved by
means of their hinges, and certain square plates of metal. He
afterwards placed his mirrors in the midst of the solar rays, pre-
cisely at noonday. The rays of the sun being reflected by this
mirror, he kindled a dreadful fire in the ships, which were reduced
to ashes, at a distance equal to that of a bow-shot.—*Tzetzes,
Chiliad,* II. 119.

struction of the lenses. These accomplished, he commenced to build his great mirror. It was composed
of 168 pieces of plain silvered glass, six inches by eight
in size, and he required to examine above 500 pieces
before the most perfect could be obtained. Between
each was an interval of four lines, to allow a free
motion, and to permit the observer to see the place,
to which the images were to be thrown. The
whole were mounted in an iron frame, so fitted
with screws and springs, that a motion could be
given to them in any direction, and the images
reflected from all the mirrors easily thrown upon
the same spot. In eight experiments, he obtained the following results, which clearly show the
possibility of setting fire to the Roman fleet:—On
March 23d, a plank of tarred beech was set on fire at
sixty-six feet, with only forty mirrors, and without
the mirror being put upon its stand. On the same
day, a plank tarred and sulphured, and having the
mirror more disadvantageously placed, was fired, at
the distance of 126 feet, with 98 mirrors. On the 3d
of April, at four o'clock in the evening, a slight inflammation was made upon a plank covered with wool
cut into small pieces, distant 138 feet, with 112 mirrors.
The next day, at eleven o'clock forenoon, 154 mirrors,
at the distance of 150 feet, made a tarred plank smoke
to such a degree in two minutes, that it would have
been inflamed had not the sun disappeared. On the
5th April, a dull day, at three o'clock afternoon, 154

mirrors, at a distance of 250 feet, inflamed in two minutes and a half, minute chips of deal, sulphured and
mixed with charcoal. When the sun was vivid, the inflammation took place in a few seconds. On the 10th
April, after mid-day, with a clear sun, 128 mirrors, at
the distance of 150 feet, set fire to a tarred plank of fir ;
the inflammation being very sudden. Same day, at
half-past two, 148 mirrors, at 150 feet, fired a plank
of beech sulphured in some parts, and in others covered with wool cut into small pieces ; the inflammation
was so sudden and violent that it was necessary to
plunge the plank into water in order to extinguish it.
April 11, twelve mirrors, at twenty feet, inflamed
small combustible matters ; forty-five, at twenty feet,
melted a large pewter flask that weighed six pounds ;
and 117 made some thin pieces of silver and iron red-
hot. Having satisfied himself upon this point, he followed out the subject, and constructed mirrors upon
various plans. Perhaps the most remarkable were
those formed by bending glass upon moulds of a sphe-
rical form by means of a furrow ; he was thus able
to make them of very considerable size, but they required great caution in the cooling and grinding afterwards ; and, out of twenty-four which he made, only
three were able to be preserved. One of these, forty-
six inches in diameter, was presented to the King of
France, and was regarded as the most powerful burning mirror in Europe.

A few years before the commencement of these experiments, Buffon succeeded to M. Du Fay in the office of Intendant to the Royal Garden and Cabinet, and, as before hinted, this appointment ultimately fixed his mind to the pursuits of natural history. He was only thirty-two years of age; and when he saw such a mass of materials at his command, a great part of which was unnoticed by any naturalist, we may easily conceive that a mind possessed of such enthusiasm, would be led again to a science which it had previously studied; and he entered eagerly into its details, calling to his assistance, in some departments where he was deficient, the talents of men who were capable and worthy of the association. The great work now contemplated, was intended to embrace every branch of the animal kingdom; but he thought that it would be incomplete, unless the composition of the globe which sustained such a multitude of living creatures, should itself be first elucidated, and it was accordingly commenced by a history or theory of the earth, which he afterwards augmented by what he termed the " Epochas of Nature." The first volume of the Natural History of Quadrupeds did not appear till 1749, ten years after his appointment as Intendant of the Gardens; and the first edition of the whole work was not completed till 1767, occupying its author during a period of sixteen years. Year after year he also wished to render it more complete; he endeavoured to keep pace with the science and its discoveries, and we find an additional supplementary volume published

in 1782, only six years before his death, and when
he began to feel very severely the tortures of a painful malady. During the progress of the work, he
appears also to have kept up that unremitting perseverance which characterises the pursuits of his earlier
years, and he is said to have employed fourteen hours
daily in writing and study, until compelled by pain to
limit his exertions.

Previous to the publication of the first volume of
his Natural History, Buffon was enabled to increase
his domestic felicity, by a marriage with a lady with
whom he had been for some time acquainted. In 1752,
he married Mademoiselle Saint Belin, who, though
without fortune, possessed qualifications which rendered the happiness of her husband undoubted. She
eagerly followed the train of honours which was now
brightly expanding upon him, and watched every
step which he gained with fresh anxiety; many
years seem thus to have been passed in great tran-
quillity, and present an unvaried routine of research
and addition to the works which were advancing.
During the height of this bright career, he was honour-
ed with marks of approbation by many of the sove-
reigns of Europe, and by the learned societies of his
country. In 1771, Louis XIV. conferred upon him
the distinction of erecting his estate into a Comptè;
and, inviting him to Fontainbleau, wished him to
accept the office of Administrator of the Forests in his
dominions, which Buffon however refused.

During his whole life he enjoyed a singular portion of good health, notwithstanding the irregularities which all his biographers allow that he frequently indulged in. He was afflicted late in life with the stone, which, about his seventy-second or seventy-third year, became extremely annoying and painful. He would not submit to an operation, and certainly accelerated his death by his obstinacy, as his medical attendants, on an after examination, affirmed, that he would have been safely relieved by an easy operation. Under all the sufferings of this painful disease, he is said to have assiduously continued his studies ; and it may be remarked, as confirming this assertion, that with all men who have studied long and perseveringly, the act becomes confirmed to a habit, and instead of being irksome, in their greater pains and imbecilities, becomes an amusement to the mind, and a solace to their bodily frailties. We are accustomed too often to couple study with what is disagreeable.

Buffon continued for nearly eight years in severe affliction : he retained his reason till within a few hours of his death, but sunk under excruciating torture, on the 16th April 1788, in the eighty-first year of his age. Upon dissection, fifty stones were found in his bladder. His body was embalmed and conveyed to Montbard, to be placed, according to his directions, in the same vault with that of his wife. Every earthly honour was paid to his memory: a concourse of academicians, and of persons of rank and distinction, at-

tended the funeral: above 20,000 people were assembled
to see it pass: a monument was erected to his memory;
and though there is much to blame in the private
character of Buffon, his name as a naturalist will
long continue to be remembered.

Buffon left one son who inherited considerable abilities, and appears to have been fondly attached to his
parent. He entered the army, and rose to the rank
of major in the regiment of Angoumois. He was destined, however, to live in a more unsettled period, and
during the Revolution was condemned to death, and
perished on the scaffold. The abilities of the father
were no safeguard for the son; nor was the utility
of his own works, or his kindness during life to his
retainers, a greater protection afterwards to his own
remains, against the ruthless hands of popular fury.
The hatred to the noblesse and aristocracy of France
was borne by so violent a tide, that the remains of
this illustrious naturalist were torn up and left un-
buried, the leaden coffin carried off, his monument
razed to the ground, and this, by part of the same
20,000 spectators who had formerly attended the
mournful procession to the grave !*

* A citizen who loved the sciences, and who, indignant at the
profanation of genius, went to Paris to complain of it, and proposed
to the Committee of Public Instruction to place Buffon in the
Pantheon. This attempt, however, was unavailing, and the Committee were unanimously of opinion, that the place would be
profaned by the presence of a man who was connected, like

The personal appearance of Buffon is said to have
been commanding, while his countenance was intelli-
gent. The engravings which we have seen, represent
his forehead high and ample, but we should scarcely
say that his countenance was very prepossessing. His
gait was erect, but perhaps leaned a little more to the
strut of foppery, than to a mein of dignity. In his disposition he seems to have been zealous and perseve-
ring, and to have followed out all his undertakings
with great ardour. The study of a subject, so as to
acquire its mastery, must however have cost him
considerable labour ; and he was always inclined to be
led away by beauties or defects, which a lively power
of imagination presented. This we can every where
trace in his writings ; by the best judges they have
been pronounced elegant, but more attention is always
given to the style and detail as it were, of the story,
than to that rigid adherence to truth which is so
essentially required by the naturalist. This may be
preserved without dry and weary detail, and at the
same time without wandering theoretically from the
subject. Nature presents innumerable instances, where
there is no need of any embellishment, beyond the garb
in which she has already dressed them, and where the
gaudy trickery of language is unnecessary, to give additional lustre to her beautiful but chaste productions.

Notwithstanding the high reputation of his works,

Buffon, with the aristocracy of the country.—*Brewst. Encyclop.*
Art. Buffon.

and the very large proportion of time which was devoted to study, Buffon appeared to little advantage
in company. His conversation did not reach beyond
mediocrity, and the time at table was spent in light
talk, exceeding even the licensed freedoms of the
French. The power of communicating information
was either wanting, or reserved for his particular
friends in private, and he considered that a discussion
upon the Sciences should be confined to books alone.
These opinions may have influenced his wish for comparative privacy, and it is certain that he did not mingle
with his contemporaries in literary and scientific fame.

Vanity has been generally allowed to be the greatest failing in the mind of Buffon, and the pains
which he took to work up his writings, and his severe
study, have perhaps been too often invidiously re-
ferred " to the consideration of what after generations
would think regarding him." He delighted in reading aloud his own works to his visitors, and chiefly
those which he considered his finest pieces. Parts
of the Natural History of Man, the description of
the Deserts of Arabia in the History of the Camel,
that of the Swan, &c.,* were his favourites. It is but
justice to say, however, that a more laudable inducement to recite them, than the mere love of hearing them
praised, has been assigned by some of his biographers.

* Buffon read the last article to Prince Henry of Prussia, when
he visited him at Montbard ; and, as a mark of his delight, the
Prince sent Buffon a service of porcelain, on which swans were
represented in every attitude.—*Brewst. Encyclop. Art. Buffon.*

" They were read with the view of hearing opinions and receiving corrections;" he willingly received any hint of improprieties of style, and was open to imperfections when pointed out to him. It is not so certain that an opinion of pieces recited in this way was always given with that candour which would allow correction.

He delighted also in what was luxurious or magnificent, and was devoted to his dress almost to the extreme of foppery. He spent much time at his toilet, and even in his latest years had his hair dressed and powdered twice, or three times daily. Every Sunday he exhibited himself after service to the peasantry of Montbard, dressed in a rich lace garment, and attended by his son and principal retainers.

In the private character of Buffon, we regret there is not much to praise; his disposition was kind and benevolent, and he was generally beloved by his inferiors, followers, and dependents, which were numerous over his extensive property; he was strictly honourable, and was an affectionate parent. In early youth he had entered into the pleasures and dissipations of life, and licentious habits seem to have been retained to the last. But the great blemish in such a mind was his declared infidelity; it presents one of those exceptions among the persons who have been devoted to the study of Nature; and it is not easy to imagine a mind apparently with such powers, scarcely acknowledging a Creator, and when noticed, only by an arraignment for what appeared wanting or defective in his great works So openly, indeed, was the freedom of his religious opinions expressed, that the indignation of the Sorbonne was provoked. He had to enter into an explanation which he in some way rendered satisfactory; and while he afterwards attended to the outward ordinances of religion, he considered them as a system of faith for the multitude, and regarded those most impolitic who openly opposed them.

Painful as a detail of such opinions must be, it is the duty of every biographer to mention them ; and our readers may compare the splendid talents and humble piety of the subject of our first memoir, with the highly cultivated mind, the bright abilities of the present, but where they were coupled with the disavowment of the Being from whom all these precious gifts were derived.

The works by which Buffon is now best known, are those upon Natural History. The first of these, " Natural History, General and Particular," was completed in 1767, and amounted to fifteen volumes quarto, thirty-one octavo ; in the anatomical department he was assisted by M. D'Aubenton, and a supplementary volume afterwards appeared. This contained only the Natural History of Quadrupeds. On account of his illness, the first volumes of the History of Birds did not appear till 1771 ; in which he was assisted by M. Gueneau de Montbeillard, and in the three last he received help from the Abbé Beron.

They form nine volumes. He afterwards published a volume containing the "Natural History of Minerals," and several supplementary additions; and he intended to have added the History of Vegetables. The whole of these have been published in thirty-eight volumes 4to., or sixty-two 12mo.; of which several translated editions have appeared in this country. His other works, some of which we mentioned before, were the translation of "Hales's Vegetable Statics," "Newton's Fluxions," a "Treatise on Accidental Colours," with various papers in the "Memoirs of the Royal Academy of Sciences at Paris, from the year 1737 to 1742."

ELOGE ON BUFFON.

ELOGE ON BUFFON.

BY

P. L. COURIER,

(ADDRESSED TO HIS FELLOW CITIZENS).

— ·

I AM apprehensive lest the name of a soldier, at the head of such a subject as this, should surprise you, and appear out of its proper place; for, it may not meet your approbation, that at the very time when a new war demands all the energies of the army, of which I form a part, I should apply myself to studies which usually presuppose leisure, and which always require considerable reflection. You may blame me, called as I am to other duties, and ill fitted either to give or to conceive hopes of success, for engaging in attempts which you encourage in those young literary aspirants whom the public distinguishes among your disciples, and whom they expect to preserve the arts which you have transmitted to them. Perhaps you may even think that a man appointed, by the state, to serve his country,

not by the pen but by the sword, not in its councils but
in the field of battle, not by persuasion but by force,
has no other employments to attend to than such as
secure for our armies a superiority over other nations;
that, in a word, all the knowledge a warrior needs, is
how to obey, to fight, and to die.

You might, therefore, dissuade me from an art in
which, I flatter myself, my earliest attempts would obtain from you a favourable consideration. Far from
being indifferent to my embarrassment, in a department
where you both give instructions as masters, and award
prizes as judges, you will scarcely pardon me for having
presumed to enter upon it; and what I believed to be
an additional claim to your indulgence, may draw upon
me your censure. However severe that may be, I submit to it without murmuring; but do not condemn me
without a hearing, that I may at least endeavour to
mitigate a judgment the severity of which I dread.

From the period of life when I began to exercise my
faculties, I had a desire for instruction, and a passion
for study. I may appeal to all the superiors under
whom I have served; to all the soldiers whom I have
commanded; to all those whom I have either followed
or accompanied, or guided in the toils of war, to testify
to the fact, that these peaceable occupations never for
an instant interfered with my obedience, or diverted
my attention from the most trifling orders I had occasion either to receive or to give.

But without insisting more on my own conduct, you

surely do not suppose that the arts, literature—in a
word, philosophy, run contrary to the obligations which
society imposes, or render one of those who cultivate
them less fit or ready to serve his country, since the
knowledge which they teach, above all others, is attention to duties. But you may imagine, that tastes of this
kind are fitted only for those whose public and private
duties leave them sufficient time to devote to the cultivation of them. What profession affords more leisure
than that of arms? All others occupy, without intermission, those employed in them. The public are engaged in disputes with the lawyer every hour of his
life. The speculations of commerce leave to the mer-
chant neither pleasures free from anxiety, nor peaceable sleep; and the labourer never interrupts the circle
of his toils. The soldier is not always engaged in
fighting. His action, being most violent, is most frequently suspended. His times of rest, moreover, leave
him exempt from the thousand cares which other men
never lay aside, and the most laborious of all occupations then becomes the most idle. Is it supposed, that
in these intervals of valuable liberty, when the soldier
can follow such occupations as suit his fancy, study
would prove more dangerous and hurtful to his duties
than the pleasures in which he is every where permitted
to indulge? How many could I name, who, unknown
to all those whose habits differ so widely from theirs,
owe to such an employment of their time and leisure, a
correctness in the service, a steadiness in their labours,

a stability of heart which nature does not give; confidence in their chiefs, the love of their companions, and regard for each other! Their studies are pursued in silence, and the source of their judicious conduct escapes less attentive eyes; for they love science, not for parade but for usefulness. Satisfied with being learned rather than appearing so, some learn from history how to judge of men and events; others, in calculation and the abstractions of the higher departments of geometry, rise to the most sublime efforts of the human mind. Others still (for many different routes lead to wisdom) take the works of nature for their study, and conceive a taste, or rather a passion for this pursuit, which never becomes extinct in the heart where it has once been kindled by the eloquence of Buffon. The mention of this name reminds me of all the difficulties of my undertaking. I apprehend, however, that if you consent to throw a glance at these sketches of a hand which cannot be much exercised, you will not think me inexcusable, for having selected, from among the subjects you proposed to the meeting, that least suited to my powers. And why? Because I intend to praise only what appears to me most deserving of praise. I shall be silent as to the rest. To speak of my inability would be to suppose, either that you cannot perceive it, or that you do not hold me accountable for it.

When the works of Newton appeared, they were received in Europe with a kind of distrust; for, whether it was that he disdained to make himself intelligible to

minds less elevated than his own, or that, forgetting
too much his own superiority, he fancied he was sufficiently explicit when he understood himself; no one at
first comprehended him, and some of his countrymen
scarcely guessed at his meaning. But his discoveries
were discussed by the learned, and each day they were
made clearer, even by the objections of those who com-
bated them; accordingly, they soon produced a great
revolution in the sciences, which England and Germany
recognised, while France still hesitated to submit to it,
and blushed to receive instruction from a rival. The
correct sciences do not readily tolerate these discussions.
The severity of their methods, and the clearness of the
principles on which they are founded, seem to render it
necessary that every proposition should be admitted
without difficulty, or rejected without hesitation; but
the kind of obscurity which Newton had either thrown
over his writings, or at least left upon them, indicating
his proofs rapidly, or disdaining to give them at all,
dissatisfied those who held to the old laws, and, by
authorizing doubts, served at least as a pretext for the
contradictions which these new ideas at first encoun-
tered. Few people were anxious to understand an
author who appeared to have no wish to be understood.
This resistance, however, could not be long continued.
People soon passed from one extreme to the other.
The greater part of those theories which Newton had
given without demonstration, having had the requisite
evidence supplied by other hands, what was not proved

became probable, and from that time admiration held
all in subjection; his name alone was a sufficient demonstration; every thing seemed proved by the words,
He has said it!

It was, if I am not deceived, in these circumstances,
when this kind of deviation, which Newton at first inspired us with was converted into enthusiasm, that
Buffon translated the Treatise on Fluxions. And here
I cannot avoid making a reflection, which has often
occurred to me when reading his other works; and
which, according to the idea I have retained of them,
does not at the present time appear to me far from the
truth. In these somewhat severe studies, by which,
unquestionably, the first fire of ardent genius should
have been tamed, may it not have happened that the
form in which these new calculations were then presented, offering to his mind ideas of infinity in every
order, may have easily seduced his imagination, for
which, afterwards, a world scarcely afforded sufficient
materials for description; and which, even although
sobered by age, and corrected by observation, too often
still overleaped the bounds of truth and even of possibility? If other more solid reasons contributed, as we
must suppose, to fix his attention on this branch of
mathematics, we may imagine that these deceptive, but,
at the same time, new and grand images, flattered his
mind and decided his choice; the more especially as
another individual, in the same age, was attracting
admiration by the brilliancy and graces of his mind,

seduced and abused by these illusions, having devoted
to this matter a lost work, running astray in the infini-
tesimal metaphysics, without being able to confine himself to the exactitude of these sciences, or to impart to
them the charms of his imagination. But Fontenelle
wished to make a book, Buffon merely to make known
that of Newton. The kind of reputation for which he
seemed destined, not being to enrich the sciences by
discoveries, but to render them attractive by his elo-.
quence; I regret that I am unable to speak here, in
any detail, respecting the works of his youth, and to
show by what labours he amassed the profuse wealth
he afterwards showed in his writings. Not that I think
his eloge incomplete without these details, which perhaps would have been sufficient of themselves to render
any other name famous, but which will scarcely be
missed in the life of Buffon. But however useless as
regards his reputation, they are by no means so in
reference to general instruction; and if it be only by
following the example of celebrated men we can hope
to come up to them, or even surpass them (a necessary
ambition to enable us to attain to what is great); it is
not to be doubted, that the only torch which can en-
lighten and sustain so noble an emulation, is the attentive observation of the progress by which they reached
an elevation which separates them from other men.
Fortunate are those who can thus follow, and meditate
on all the steps of Buffon's progress, and who, finding
in his attempts important lessons for themselves, show

us how his pen learned the art of painting nature in a
style equal to the subject. As for myself, I cannot
enter upon these useful researches, because I am separated from all the monuments of literature, as well as
from the small number of individuals, who having lived
with these heroes of a past age, yet retain some recol-
lection of them. In what I have to say of Buffon, I
can only consult my memory, full, as it is, of his great
works, but silent as to his life. The extent of his reputation is scarcely known to me; and such, in a word, is
the disadvantage of my position, that having to cele-
brate a man whose name is already too great for a voice
like mine, I am reduced to the necessity of being unable
to praise in him any thing but what is expressly above
all praise. I must, however, speak to you of his immortal work. The further I advance with my subject,
the more does my courage fail me; and notwithstanding the law I imposed on myself when commencing a
task, the importance of which alarmed me, I cannot
avoid to remind you again of my incompetency, and to
solicit your indulgence.

If I were referring to this magnificent work under
the different aspects in which it may be regarded, and
holding up to admiration a genius which showed its
superiority in every department where it was called
upon to excel, in order to succeed in my attempt, this
discourse would not only exceed the limits you have
prescribed to me, but would form a work of considerable extent; for there is no kind of knowledge which

the human mind is capable of cultivating; no science,
art, or even trade or profession, having to do with the
wants or conveniences of life, which has not either an
intimate connection with, or an obvious relation to the
vast science named Natural History; and the study of
which, consequently, more or less attentively, is not indispensable to any one who pretends to give a complete
system. Now, in each of these departments, a detailed
examination of one of Buffon's books, would enable us
every where to perceive, in its author, the man of genius
or the man of taste; or rather, by this kind of analysis,
we would discover many great men in Buffon alone.
But even though I were permitted, in a mere essay like
this, to make use of such divisions, or others less multiplied, I should venture to avoid them; for such extensive and varied kinds of knowledge, the union of which
in one individual was almost inconceivable, but yet
necessary to explain and describe the whole of nature,
are every where found in this work so closely connected,
that they can scarcely be separated even in thought;
to distinguish them in this manner would prevent us
feeling all the admiration which Buffon ought to in-
spire, as it is their assemblage that is the most admir-
able mark of the sublimity of his genius; but in other
respects his own example teaches us how to regard
him. It is from himself that we must learn to measure
objects so great as his genius. Let us avoid, then,
while praising him, the methods which he himself despised. Let us attempt to look on him as he looked on

nature, not in the hope of painting it with his own
colours; but as impossible to seize in any other manner; and without wishing to decompose all the rays of
his glory; without separating the writer from the naturalist, the orator, and, if you please, the poet from
the philosophical observer. Let us endeavour to take
a glance at his work, which will give an idea, not of
each part, but of the whole. Let us examine, in general, what must have been the object of the author,
and how he fulfilled that object; what he wished to do
and what he really did.

If his design had been only to give us a book where
all the known productions of nature should be deli-
neated, the greatness of this undertaking, of itself,
would astonish us, and make us admire the boldness of
a mind capable of such an idea; for in each class of
the objects which natural history considers, a small
number of species has sometimes been sufficient to
occupy the whole life of laborious observers. Many
observers have acquired a just celebrity, by confining
their investigations to a single branch of the sciences
which are all here treated of; and rarely is an individual found, whose mind could embrace all the parts of
study to which he devoted himself. It is a boldness,
therefore, well worthy of admiration, to regard at once
all the beings composing the universe, and to conceive the plan, by observing their infinite varieties,
of becoming acquainted with and describing them all.
Buffon desired to do even more than this. The bodily

powers of man are estimated by what he performs;
those of the mind by what he undertakes. In order to
form an idea of the immensity of the work in which
Buffon engaged, it is sufficient to consider, that the first
objects to which men would direct attention (as soon as
the establishment of societies and laws, securing the
means of easy subsistence, permitted them to entertain
other ideas than such as related to the wants of life).
must necessarily have been the works of nature, with
whose magnificence they were surrounded, and which
presented themselves to their view on every side. Those
who were disposed to contemplation, having readily
remarked the principal phenomena of universal harmony, and the most obvious properties of organised
matter; this first glance, though without reflection, on
the picture of nature, immediatedly inspired, by the
surprise it excited, curiosity to penetrate deeper, and
become acquainted with details; and hence men began
to observe, to travel, and to write; but travellers and
writers could not all be enlightened men. If it sometimes happened, that an individual of sense and judgment travelled, for the sake of acquiring knowledge,
how many others, ill instructed, credulous, superstitious,
untruthful, whom accident, necessity, or cupidity, carried far from their native country, brought back from
unknown regions a thousand fables for one fact, and
whose faithless and inaccurate narrations were compiled
without the least discernment! Accordingly, in proportion as useful remarks became multiplied, confounded.

and buried in the mass of compilations and narratives
which multiplied still more; the difficulty of collecting
them continually increased along with the distaste which
always accompanies work of this kind; for, as may
have been noticed in these writings, whatever may be
the style, the curiosity natural to man for all that treats
of remote objects, often holds the place of that interest
which art alone can impart to other works; and it was
easy, therefore, for people to persuade themselves, that
in order to be an observer, naturalist, author, and at
the same time secure readers, nothing was henceforth
necessary but to run and to write. No one went away,
for however short a distance, from his birth-place,
without thinking that he was called upon to publish at
least letters to a friend; and, even such as undertook
more important tasks, abused the indulgence of the
public, anxious as they were for instruction, by describing, in detail, the most trifling events of their progress, life, conversations, and sometimes even their love
intrigues. All this increased the labour of the savant;
who, reading not so much for himself as for others, and
fearing to overlook some circumstance worthy of being
noted, saw himself condemned to follow throughout a
narrative encumbered with so much useless matter.

The existing knowledge respecting Natural History,
when Buffon took up his pen, was scattered in the manner described, throughout a multitude of books, or
rather, it may be said, in every book, since there is
scarcely any one which does not owe some tribute to

this science, and that of nature became intelligible by
means of commentaries. So many ill-digested writings,
which men of science themselves perused with difficulty,
had not only to be read, but studied, by Buffon; and
he required to make himself acquainted with all that
men had thought up to his time, in order to mark, on
the same plan, the whole series of truths and errors.
But he was by no means one of those authors, whose
merit, confined to giving a faithful account of the ideas
or discoveries of their predecessors, obtains rather the
gratitude than the admiration of the public.

Could a genius such as his undertake the troublesome
task of collecting all that others knew, if it had not
been for the purpose of adding to it all of which they
were ignorant? It is in this respect, that we may say
his ambition was without bounds. He wished to become acquainted with all that the earth encloses in its
bowels, to search the depths of the sea, to penetrate to
places where light never comes; he wished to describe
all that the surface of the earth lays open to the sun;
and, ascending in imagination to the celestial spaces,
to obtain a glimpse of the designs of the Supreme Intelligence. But what do I say? He was not content-
ed to unveil to men the secrets of the earth, the beauties
of nature, and the order of the universe; he even
aspired to the power of teaching us how these wonders
were produced; how they will one day perish; when
they were created, and what will still be their dura-
tion; in a word every thing which the immensity of

time and space removes even from our conjectures.
His work, finished on the plan in which it was conceived, would have been the history of the world and
the plan of creation; and it would not have been his
fault, if human curiosity, so vague in its desires, had
not been satisfied.

But if this undertaking was, as cannot be doubted,
the greatest which even Buffon could conceive; on the
other hand, the means he had to execute it were such
that no past time could have been more favourable to
success; and never could one who exerted himself to
extend the empire of human knowledge enjoy an opportunity of using such vast and multiplied resources.
The world was then at peace, and this allowed observers, however distantly separated, to carry on their
labours conjointly; or the wars that did arise, of little
importance in themselves, and interesting only to kings,
did not prevent nations from favouring, by common
consent, useful and learned investigations, interesting
to the whole human race. The commerce of knowledge
was always free; and protected sometimes by the enemies of all commerce and of all relation between states.
Did not an instance occur, of cases addressed to Buffon,
remaining untouched in a vessel plundered by pirates,
and, in the disorder of general pillage, the seal of philosophy being held sacred even by those who profess to
have a respect for nothing? Universal oppression left
no other mode of employing their understandings free
to men, save the study of the arts and sciences; no

other object of curiosity than their productions and
their discoveries; no other hope of distinction, than that
which cannot be arrested from talents acquired by long
continued labours. But what do I say? Even tyranny
itself, as blind as it is inconstant, thought to conceal
from the people its weakness and injustice, by turning
their attention to another object, even to that philosophy which ought to have overthrown it; and the
sciences derived this advantage from the common servi-
tude, that no division among the nations, united under
the same chain, brought any opposition to their progress.

To these advantages, which Buffon owed to the times
in which he wrote, were joined others even more important, which were peculiar to himself; for that happy
facility which men of science enjoyed for bringing their
observations and discoveries to a common centre, might
have been rendered unavailing for the perfection of his
work, if the pretensions, jealousy, and hatred, of too
frequent occurrence among them, had been opposed to
the union of their knowledge and talents. But Buffon
knew well how to subdue these passions, so fatal to
every kind of success in great undertakings. The ascen-
dency of his genius subjected all other minds to his,
and brought, so to speak, under his direction, all those
who had cultivated any one department of knowledge
relating to his subject. His name, alone, was enough
to check the factious in literature; and those who, as
philosophers, sometimes refused to acknowledge him as

their master, seduced and attracted by his eloquence, soon brought, of their own accord, all that they were able to furnish him. The materials thus coming into him on all sides, he seemed to employ nothing more than his voice in the construction of his edifice.

In fact, throughout the whole of Europe, it may even be said throughout the whole world, all philosophers and men of observation, travellers going to a distance to interrogate nature, and observers more limited in their scope; and also, on their side, all people in office, ministers, and kings themselves; all those, in short, who were in a condition, either by knowledge or power, to second such a work, devoted themselves to Buffon. Some of them lent the assistance of their talents, others of their authority. Hence, without ever leaving his cabinet, he had the means of collecting a greater number of observations, and acquiring a greater amount of knowledge, than the longest journeys would have furnished him with. All parts of the globe, accessible to the industry or curiosity of Europeans, became, as it were, present to his eyes. All he wished to know was described or painted by the most skilful hands; every thing he wished to see was transported across mountains and seas. Any fact which might appear new, an interesting remark or discovery, in whatsoever part of the earth accident or research had given rise to it, was instantly treasured up and communicated to Buffon by a multitude of individuals, jealous to deserve what would distinguish them, and whose names a stroke of

his pen would preserve from oblivion; for it was never
doubted that every thing he wrote would be immortal!
And is it to be wondered at, that when such finished
pictures were seen growing under his hand, it should
have been conceived, that they were destined to endure
and be admired, as long as men were alive to the
charms of eloquence and the beauties of nature? The
most valuable productions of another kind have their
course and allotted destiny. Whatever may be the
degree of perfection which poetry can attain, its productions require to be renewed; that which, in one age,
moved rocks, in another is scarcely listened to by men.
History becomes old still more rapidly; every day new
facts efface those of the preceding day. In a word, we
may expect to see every composition, whose merit or
conception belongs to the things which time alters or
destroys, become gradually more obscure, and at last
fall into oblivion. But, before the writings of Buffon
can undergo such a fate, or the value of his pictures be
misunderstood, it is necessary that Nature herself should
change; that the lion should lose his fierceness of character, the dog his intelligence and fidelity, the eagle
the empire of the air, the Arab his independence, or
that Man should forget Nature; for, so long as his
eyes are directed to it, the grandeur and variety of the
spectacle it presents, will never fail to recall the only
genius whose view could take in the whole extent of it,
and who had the art to describe the details of it.

I am not unaware, at the same time, of what has

been said on this subject, and what enlightened men
still allege, that there can be nothing truly estimable
in a work on the sciences but what is useful to the
learned; that this utility consists in discovering new
truth; or at least in presenting, in a new order, and
such as is fitted to facilitate their study, truths already
known; that the didactic style, that is to say, the style
peculiar to the sciences, is from its nature the simplest
and humblest of all, never having any other object but
to offer a clear sense to the mind, nor any greater
merit than not to be remarked; that, in such cases, all
emphasis in expression only annoys a reader who is in
search of truth, and by giving false and confused ideas
to such individuals as are less correctly instructed, in-
jures the progress of the sciences; that far from being
able to derive from oratorical ornament and parade of
language, any real utility, the greater part of them owe
their existence to the invention of certain signs, which
supply entire phrases, and are brought to perfection
only in proportion as they have learned to dispense
with words; that eloquence, the enemy of accuracy, intended to move or to seduce, accustomed to hurry the
passions impetuously forward, and even in its calmest
moments, less occupied with truth than with verisimili-
tudes, is a stranger to every work whose object is not
to persuade but to convince; that philosophy instructs
but does not harangue!

But what are we to infer from all this? Is it meant
to lay an interdict on all that can make instruction

agreeable, and render it, by the allurements of a polished language, not more useful, but more attractive?
Since, in addressing men, it is necessary to employ the
words and expressions in use among men, why not
choose what is best fitted to secure their attention and
favourable regard? Truth, you say, needs no ornament;
every thing which adorns conceals it. Paint her then
naked but beautiful; let her strike our attention and
please our taste at the same time. Is it enough to
make her known, if we do not make her loved? Those
sciences, even, which profess the severest exactitude,
presenting only irresistible evidence, and which would
blush to sacrifice to the graces, are not without their
degree of elegance. In subjecting the mind to the force
of its proofs, it does not disdain to flatter it by a certain
address. If, indeed, there are studies which no charm
embellishes, and departments of knowledge which no
thing can reconcile with taste, those who cultivate them
are much to be pitied. But we find more to delight us
when occupied with nature. Like herself, mother of
all the arts, there is no art foreign to the sciences, of
which she is the object. Eloquence owes to her its life
and attractions; and such is the unchangeable relation
subsisting between them, that we can say nothing
eloquent which is not found in Nature, nor make a true
image of Nature which is not eloquent. The beauties
of the one are those of the other; all their treasures
are common. Accordingly, to attempt to separate them,
is to contradict the essence of things; and to pretend to

exclude eloquence from the descriptions of Nature, is to
deprive the painter of the use of colours.

But every one judges by what he feels; and the same
objects do not make the same impressions on all. Accordingly, among men who study to acquire a knowledge
of Nature, all have not the same manner of regarding it
nor of delineating it. Those who contemplate it without enthusiasm describe it methodically, measuring
every thing scrupulously, halting at every point, and
exerting all their attention to seize even the smallest
traits. Whatever beauty is presented to them, their
heart remains untouched! The greatest magnificence
in the adornments of the universe affords them nothing
but names to be classified, tables to be drawn up, cold
enumerations to deduce and compare. Their view,
unceasingly occupied in these toilsome labours, never
reposes on smiling images, and they find, every where
in Nature, the same details to draw out, the same task
to fulfil. But as soon as a mind of some elevation applies itself to contemplate it, the multitude of sublime
ideas to which it gives rise, transport it out of itself;
and without thinking of being a poet, it becomes so by
expressing what it sees and feels! Which of the two
represent Nature best? The one employs the eye and
the pencil, the other the rule and the compass. The
one gives a grand and picturesque view, the other a
dry and minute plan. Is, then, the most faithful picture that which offers to the eye the dimensions of
objects, measured exactly, but without perspective and

without colour; or that which produces in the spectator
the same ideas, the same sensations, the same emotions
as its model? And who does not experience, in reading
Buffon, that the heart, seduced by the illusions of an
enchanting style, imagines that it sees Nature herself
in his descriptions, and feels, in effect, all the impressions which its actual presence would produce? Those
who study them with taste, never open, without a certain degree of veneration, the book where Nature is
represented in all its magnificence; and the more the
mind is accustomed to meditate on these master-pieces,
the more is it gratified to find it again represented, so
majestic and sublime, in the pictures of Buffon. But
however strange one may be to knowledge of this description, it is sufficient to have some share of that
intelligence and sensibility of which few are destitute,
joined to the most common notions of all that the least
attentive eye remarks in Nature; it is enough to see
and to feel, to recognise in Buffon all that Nature offers
of what is grandest and most majestic. Where is the
man, so indifferent to every kind of beauty, as not
sometimes to have experienced, while traversing forests,
pausing on the slope of a mountain, or viewing the ex-
panse of the sea from an elevated beach, this inexpres-
sible feeling of admiration, and the idea which then
springs up in the mind of the variety of beings and the
immensity of the universe? Is there any one whom the
view of the beautiful nights of summer does not delight,
and throw into a state of tranquil meditation, or who

can prevent himself sinking into a silent revery, when
the darkening sky and the hollow sound of the waves
announce the approach of a tempest? And can it be
otherwise, than that so many wonders, the view of
which throws a contemplative heart into admiration;
and which, when spread over nature, make such deep
impressions on the coarsest senses, should strike and
dazzle, when assembled in a work where the enthusiasm
inseparable from the subject is joined to the charm of
illusion?

Buffon brings before his readers the objects which
are known to them, as if they were present to their
view, and familiarises them even with those whose
entire nation is strange to them. Every thing he speaks
of is present. We transport ourselves along with him
to every place he describes. If he represents to us the
life and manners of the wild animals of our continent,
we follow him into the forests, we admire rude nature,
the silence which reigns in these solitudes, and so many
dumb objects which speak to the heart. We lament
the victim of a cruel sport, deceived by the ground,
which, in his rapid career, he scarcely touches; and we
become interested in the faithful, but not very peaceable love of a couple of Roes, which birth unites, and
death alone separates. If he paints another aspect of
nature in other climates, under the burning zones of
Africa and Asia, we fancy ourselves to be transported
to the heart of the deserts of Arabia, and distinguish,
among the hissings of reptiles, the voice of the Ono-
crotalus and the cries of the Jabiru; or we tremble at

seeing, on the banks of the Senegal, the timid Gazelle
descend to the brink of the stream where the Tiger lies
in ambush. The view of the universe, when we observe
it with less indifference than the majority of men, presents no agreeable image which Buffon does not bring
before the mind; no sombre perspective which does not
reappear in his work, where we every where perceive,
as in Nature herself, order, harmony, fertility; the re-
medy by the side of the evil; the earth prodigal of
every blessing; but, at the same time, war prevailing,
strength triumphant, and innocence sacrificed.

It is by the harmony of his eloquence, and the sweet-
ness he infuses into his expressions, that Buffon de-
lights the senses, and fixes the regard of his auditors,
even when he is speaking of animals and natural productions, the least noble in our eyes. But when a vaster
field offers itself to the flight of his genius; if he interrupts the enumeration of the species which inhabit
the earth, in order to do homage to the principles of
being and of life; or, if he begins to describe the structure of the universe, and the equilibrium of worlds
weighing the one against the other; a superior power
then raises us above the sphere of human view! It is
no longer a mortal we listen to, but Nature herself which
opens her sanctuary, and at whose voice we are obliged
to bow. Eternal Wisdom! sole object worthy of the
exertions and curiosity of man, how powerful is your
attraction over the mind that seeks to know thee; and
how happy the individual, who can devote his life to
the contemplation of thee!

THE

NATURAL HISTORY

OF

MONKEYS.

MAMMALIA.

NATURAL HISTORY OF MONKEYS.

AMONG the varied races of living beings which
inhabit this world, none perhaps have excited so
much speculation and general interest, as those to
which we have devoted our present little volume.
From the shy and retired manners of the animals
in a wild state, their habits are of difficult inves-
tigation, and would require much patience, and a
greater allowance of time, than it is often possible
for those individuals who possess the enviable opportunities to devote to them. The greater portion
of the information we possess, is therefore derived
from the accounts of travellers, too often collected
from hearsay evidence, exaggerated as the fears and
superstitions of the natives have been influenced,
and which have appeared as " dreamy forms"

" That the soul sees—and, we suppose, the eyes."

E

We are mostly aware how easily the minds of many
native tribes are wrought upon; and it can scarcely be
a matter of surprise, that traditions* should exist, with
accounts of the prowess, sagacity, or cruelty of these
creatures.   Occasional glimpses of an animal clothed
in shaggy hair, of gigantic size, with tusks rivalling
those of the largest and most ferocious beasts of prey;—
possessing a hideous resemblance of countenance and
general proportions to man, and assuming positions
somewhat human, would present to an untutored
mind, a chaos of sensations, whose impressions scarcely
could be afterwards detailed; while one of higher
cultivation might combine doubts of their animal or
human nature, and add to either the brutal or malignant qualities of both.   And it is under such influ-
ences, fear predominating, that the accounts of their
concerted attacks, their carrying off negroes for slaves,
distribution of the different sexes, and of their cruelty
and carnivorous propensities, have been handed down
with embellishments by the older historians.

In other countries, superstition exercises her influence.   India, so horribly celebrated by the sacrifices
of its infatuated devotees, is in some districts no less
so for its weak and extravagant idolatry.   In Ahme-
nadab, hospitals have been erected for the benefit
of apes, where thousands are kept in fancied ease
and indulgence; and another city, which was taken

* Such as those of the *Fesse* and *Goolocn.*

by General Goddart in 1780, upon its surrender contained forty thousand inhabitants, and as many monkeys. They are even worshipped by the Brahmins,
and are raised to the rank of gods. Gorgeous temples
are erected,

" With pious care a monkey to enshrine !"

Mofleus, in his History of India, describes one of great
magnificence—it was fronted by a portico for receiving
victims sacrificed to it, which was supported by no
less than 700 columns; and Linschotten relates, that
when the Portuguese plundered one of these monkey
palaces, in the island of Ceylon, they found, in a little
gold casket, the tooth of an ape; a relic held by the
natives in such veneration, that they offered seven
hundred thousand ducats to redeem it.—It was, however, burnt by the Viceroy, to stop the progress of
idolatry. Among the ancient Egyptians, they also
seem to have been held in more than ordinary reve-
rence, or at least to have borne a rank equal to that
of the sacred ibis. They were like them represented
in the sculptures, and their bodies were preserved as
mummies.

We cannot, however, class under such infatuation,
the idea which, even in comparatively modern times,
prevailed among men who possessed great learning,
and minds at once comprehensive and penetrating;
" that men and monkeys belonged to the same species,
and were no otherwise distinguished from each other,

than by circumstances which can be accounted for,
by the different physical or moral agencies to which
they have been exposed." *   And we can only consider them in the words of an eminent anatomist, as
" equally unacquainted with the structure and func-
tions of men and monkeys, not conversant with
zoology and physiology, and therefore entirely destitute of the principles on which alone a sound judgment can be formed, concerning the natural capabilities
and destiny of animals, as well as the laws according
to which certain changes of character, certain de-
partures from the original stock, may take place."†

Seeing, then, that the information handed down to
us regarding this singular family, has been in many
instances exaggerated and misrepresented, we shall
endeavour, in the following pages, to detail what can
be depended upon, making use of the discoveries and
researches of the modern naturalists who have travelled aware of the doubtful points, and were competent,
by their previous studies, for the task of unravelling
them ; while the anatomy of these animals, which
approach nearest in their structure to that of man,
will be taken from the able examinations which have
been made by Geoffroy Saint Hilaire, Fred. Cuvier, Dr
Trail, and Messrs Owen and Yarrel.

Modern zoologists have applied to this family, consisting of two great divisions, the title of *Quadrumanous*, or four-handed, from their generally possess-

* Monboddo, Rousseau, Lamark.   † Lawrence.

ing thumbs, or members opposable to the fingers of both the fore and hind limbs, which enables them to grasp any object firmly with either, and renders them expert climbers. The most casual stroller through a menagerie, must be immediately struck with the surprising agility, the powerful leaps and swings, and the complete gliding ease, with which all these motions are performed; and an observer in their natural abodes will soon arrive at the conclusion, that their habits are strictly arboreal, and that their economy is intimately connected with the boundless forests of the tropics. They are in fact seldom seen at any distance from woods, and the species which inhabit craggy precipices, such as those in the neighbourhood of the Cape of Good Hope, in Barbary, and about Gibraltar, deviate from the type, become more quadruped in their form and actions, and have therefore always been placed last in our systems.

Their true and natural abodes are the trackless forests, which so richly clothe the countries under the tropics, and which alike supply them with food, and protect them from the heat of those scorching climes. During the middle period of the day, these forests are filled with the animal world, courting their grateful shades, silent and resting; and it is only in some deep deep glade, "afraid to glitter in the noontide beams," that the screams of an awakened parrot, or gambols of a monkey, disturb the universal solitude. So soon, however, as a declining sun and the evening breezes reduce

the overpowering feelings, do the inhabitants of those
vast nurseries resume the exercise of their daily routine,
and none among them .occupy a more conspicuous
place than this family. The more timorous attract
the observer's attention by their endeavours of con-
cealment; and the protrusion of numerous little heads,
with bright and searching eyes, from behind the thick
boughs and foliage, plainly tells that curiosity almost
overbalances the fear of self-preservation. The more
forward again, force attention by the shower of rotten
branches, fruit, flowers, and nuts, and sometimes
materials of a less agreeable kind, that are either
directed against, or unintentionally fall near, the object
which thus attracts the attention of this prying as-
sembly; while the annoyed feelings of the spectator
soon give way to admiration, at the light and airy
gambols of those which think themselves beyond the
reach of danger, or are amused at the grimaces, and
grotesque attitudes, and half threats of those in the
immediate vicinity. This interval of activity in the
tropical forest, lasts for a comparatively short period ;
a few morning and evening hours of milder heat, are
sufficient to satisfy all their wants; the blaze of a
vertical sun, or a short twilight, again obliges them
to seek a covering from its beams, or a place of rest
and security from depredators, whose turn it now is
to satisfy the cravings of nature.

But there are some tribes inhabiting South America,
which reverse this order, and are nocturnal in their

habits. Some of the larger species remaining in complete inactivity during daylight, come forth at night, and make the forest resound with their yells and howling. Speaking of the Red Howler, an eccentric writer observes,—" Nothing can sound more dreadful than its nocturnal howlings. While lying in your hammock in those gloomy and immeasurable wilds, you hear him howling at intervals from eleven o'clock at night till daybreak. You would suppose that half the wild beasts of the forest were collecting for the work of carnage. Now it is the tremendous roar of the jaguar, as he springs on his prey ; now it changes to his terrible deep-toned growlings, as he is pressed on all sides by superior force; and now you hear his last dying moan beneath a mortal wound."*

A deep and dark evergreen, or the hollow of some decaying tree, like the " shrouded owls," are the abodes during the day of other small species ; and, when removed from their dormitory, a dreamy motion and piteous wailing, are the only exertions which announce that their rest has been disturbed, or their feelings incommoded. During the night, on the contrary, they are all energy.

The food of this family may be called almost entirely vegetable. The accounts of their love for animal food, and relish for that of human beings, as related by

* Waterton's Wanderings, 8vo edit. 305.

Neiuhoff, * can only be traced to the same sources
with the other unsubstantiated reports concerning
them, and become naturally associated, in the minds
of the inhabitants, with the hideous forms and immense tusks of the larger species. The forest will
supply them with nourishment, in the endless variety
of fruits and nuts, roots and juicy shrubs. Insects
are also greedily devoured by all, and as expertly
caught.† The stores of the wild bees furnish another
repast, and the eggs, and occasionally the young of
birds, is the only approach which can be traced to a
carnivorous propensity.

There are some accounts of the orangs feeding on
crabs and shellfish ; but we are not sure of the autho-

* " The province of Fohier hath an animal perfectly resembling
man, but longer armed, and hairy all over, called *Fesse*, most swift
and greedy after human flesh, which, that he may better take his
prey, he feigneth laughter, and suddenly, while the person stands
listening, seizeth upon him."

† A curious manner of feeding, is thus related by Ludolf in his
History of Ethiopia :—" Of apes there are infinite flocks up and
down in the mountains, a thousand and more together. There
they leave no stone unturned. If they meet with one that two
or three cannot lift, they call for more aid, and all for the sake of
the worms that lie under—a sort of diet which they relish exceedingly. They are very greedy after emmets. So that having found
an emmet hill, they presently surround it, and laying their fore
paws, with the hollow downwards, upon the ant heap, as fast as
the emmets creep into their treacherous palms, they lick them off
with great comfort to their stomachs ; and there they will lie till
there is not an emmet left."

rity whence they have been obtained. Gemelli Car.
reri tells us, that the orangs descend from the mountains when the fruits are exhausted, where they feed
on various shellfish, but particularly on a large species
of oyster. " Fearful of putting in their paws, lest
the oyster should close and crush them, they insert a
stone within the shell, which prevents it from closing,
and then drag out their prey and devour it at leisure!"

In those districts where cultivation has advanced,
they become exceedingly troublesome, and from their
numbers do no inconsiderable injury to the foreign
husbandman ; an amiable poet thus mentions their
depredations among the sugar groves :—

> " Destructive, on the upland sugar groves
> The monkey nation preys ; from rocky heights,
> In silent parties, they descend by night,
> And posting watchful sentinels, to warn
> When hostile steps approach ; with gambols, they
> Pour o'er the cane grove. Luckless he to whom
> That land pertains !"

In like manner, when a remission of watchfulness
occurs, do they plunder the maize fields, and rob the
orchards of their choicest fruits ; " they are so impu-
dent, that they will come into the gardens and eat such
sorts of fruit as grow there," says Knox;[*] and Thunberg
relates, that such is the superstitious respect in which
the Entellus monkey is held by the natives, that whatever ravages they may commit, they dare not venture

* Knox's Ceylon.

to destroy them. Emboldened by this impunity, they come down from the woods in large herds, and take possession of the husbandman's toil, with as little ceremony, as though it had been collected for their use.

In a state of confinement, vegetable diet continues their favourite and most nourishing support; but they will eat almost anything that the luxury of man has introduced, and some even become remarkable for their peculiarities. Among the greater part of them, the love of wine or diluted spirits becomes almost a passion; they are often offered as a bribe to the performance of various tricks, and they will always be greedily drunk when left within reach. Vosmaer's orang, one day when loose, commenced its exploits by finishing a bottle of Malaga wine. Happy Jerry, the ribbed nose baboon in Exeter Change, performed all his tricks upon the anticipation of a glass of gin and water; and the relish and expression with which it was taken, would have done honour to the most accomplished taster.

Nearly the whole family are gregarious,* and troops of many hundreds together may be seen in the forest glades and openings, or upon the banks of the noble rivers, which,

"Shaded and rolling on through sunless solitudes,"

form almost the only passages in those vast countries.

* *Pithecia chiropotes,* Humb., and a few other species, live in pairs.

Wherever we peruse the journeys of travellers, who have explored the interior of the tropics, we find accounts of almost innumerable bands which crowd the wooded banks, doubtless astonished at such visiters, and exhibiting every attitude and grimace, that the impulses of fear and caution can supply. In general, they live together in harmony, unless when slightly disturbed by rivalry after some favourite supply of food, in which cases, the love and knowledge of power is fully shown and exercised by the strong over their weaker companions. Intruders of any other species are either expelled, or, if too powerful, are chattered at with all their natural petulance, and stolen opportunities are watched, to pilfer the attracting store, or annoy the unwelcome aggressor.

Their breeding-places are various—cloven trees, perhaps a forsaken nest which has already reared a feathered progeny—rocks, thickets of brush, and rank grassy herbage, all afford sheltered nursing-places. The young, seldom more than two, are attended with the greatest care and anxiety by the female ; and long after they are able to follow their troop, on the approach of danger, will attach themselves to the parent, who will encounter almost anything in their defence, and who, from the utmost timidity, becomes fierce and reckless of every opponent. It is singular, however, that in confinement the very reverse most frequently takes place ; and when these animals have, with great care and attention, been

productive, the offspring was immediately left, and
the greatest apathy exhibited. Under every advantage
Frederic Cuvier was unsuccessful twice, and found it
impossible to preserve the young beyond a few hours.[*]

In geographical distribution, the quadrumanous
order presents some curious examples. That part of
them to which this volume is devoted, is found in three
divisions of the world, and is entirely confined to the
warmer parts. Europe, with one exception, which
merely skirts its southern border, and North America,
are without them, from the unsuitable nature of the
climate ; and among the various anomalous forms peculiar to New Holland, and the vast archipelago of the
Southern Ocean, scarcely one approaches to any resemblance. The smaller formed long-tailed monkeys,
(which constitute the numerous family of Guenons in
the systems,) of mild disposition and playful manners
and generally clothed with a fur of considerable beauty,
are in a general way distributed over Africa and India;
among these, however, the genus *Semnopithecus* of
F. Cuvier, seems exclusively Indian, while, with a
few exceptions, the *Cercopitheci* of the same naturalist,
and *Cercocebi* of Geoffroy, inhabit Africa. The most
typical forms in the zoology of these countries, are, in
the last ; the baboons, or *Cynocephali*, more bestial
in all their forms and habits, and deviating from
the quadrumanous type. In one or two aberrant

---

[*] The Ouistiti produced three in confinement, and nursed them
with great attention.—See our description of that species.

instances they reach India, and the Barbary ape passes
the European boundary, and may be looked on as the
extreme limit of the family in that direction. The
form again most typical to India, is seen in the long-
armed apes or Gibbons, (*Hylobates*, Illiger,) approaching the orangs somewhat in structure, found exclusively
in the islands and continent, stretching northward in
the Chinese dominions, but not existing in any land
that can be allied to the continent of Africa.

The Indian islands possess another very singular
animal in the proboscis monkey, (*Nasalis*, Geoffroy,)
which, to the form of the orangs, joins a considerable
length of tail ; but the greatest peculiarity is the shape
of the nose, which is prolonged to an extraordinary
degree, and can be compared to nothing so justly, as
some of the pasteboard masks, which may be daily
seen at the windows of our fancy toyshops. Extending our researches farther in the Asiatic continent, we
find, in the western district of China, another curious
form, furnished with long arms and tail, but of rather
graceful proportions, with a fur of rich colouring,
destitute of the bare callosities, and possessing somewhat the flattened face of the American monkeys.
It is the Chinese monkey, and constitutes Illiger's genus
Lasiopyga. Some zoologists ascribe the Island of
Madagascar as another abode of this animal, but we
strongly suspect, that, however allied in resemblance,
it will prove distinct. But the most interesting form
to these continents, is the orangs, common to both,

but in indifferent individuals ; and these, as far as our knowledge extends, confined to a very limited space : that of India inhabits almost exclusively the Island of Borneo, while the African representative is found only on the eastern coast, and particularly in Angola and Congo.

These are the principal forms inhabiting the old world ; South America possesses others of great peculiarity, and it is remarkable, that none of them can be placed in any of the African or Asiatic groups. The nostrils are always divided by a broader separation, the size and strength is much less ; in some, the proportions are very diminutive, and in a few, the habits become completely nocturnal. The inhabitants of this region, also exhibit the most perfect adaptation of structure for climbing and a silvan life, and the formation of the tail in the greater part, is a most efficient assistant in grasping and supporting themselves among the branches, and some can even introduce the extremity in the narrow parts of the bark, and withdraw from thence any small substance.* Among the Howlers, we see somewhat of the form and appearance of the baboons, which they also resemble in their larger size, their strength, and fiercer dispositions, and in the structure of the laryngeal sacks, which are connected with the os hyoides. We find, in the genus *Hapales*, an approach to the insectivorous mammaliæ, in the hooked

* Humboldt, Zool. Observations, page 329.—Description of Marimonda in present volume.

claws of the fore extremities, instead of nails; and in several of the other forms, a departure from the quadrumanous types, and a joining with the *Lemuridæ*.

As the quadrumanous races approach nearest to man in structure, and consequently in actions, it will be proper to point out some of the principal distinctions which corporeally separate them; and for this purpose, we shall confine ourselves to the two orangs, which have been universally allowed to bear the strongest resemblance. We do not intend to institute a strict comparison between the monkey and human organization, and to adduce proof from the comparison, that they are distinct as well in structure as in nature; we consider this quite unnecessary, and think that in all our systems, man should be kept entirely distinct. As he is infinitely pre-eminent by the high and peculiar character and power of his mind, and the future destination of his immaterial part, so has he been stamped with a bearing lofty and dignified, with

—— " Far nobler shape, erect and tall,
Godlike erect, with native honour clad."

We wish chiefly to illustrate, by their difference, that the parts allotted for locomotion in the most man-like monkey, are unfitted for sustaining an upright attitude, while they are beautifully adapted to perform all the requisites of a silvan life.

The first distinction that would undoubtedly strike an observer of an orang and human being placed in

the same enclosure, would be the positions and attitude; and a closer attention would soon convince, that
the corresponding members in each, while beautifully
formed for their proper uses, could not be employed
to perform similar actions, with an equal degree of
strength, firmness, or ease.

Few persons, in the present era, will assert,

> ———— " Men have four legs by nature,
> And that 'tis custom makes them go
> Erroneously upon but two."

While the fact, that no nation in the world assumes any
except the erect attitude, will be sufficiently conclusive,
without making use of the many arguments which might
be drawn from the adaptation of structure. Let us now
see how this agrees with the natural gait of the orangs.
In man, the limbs, the principal organs of progression,
and of maintaining the upright position, are equal in
length to the head and trunk together, while the
upper extremities are comparatively short. The glutei
muscles are the largest in the human body, and the
gastronemi, or calf, are of immense power, and terminate in a powerful cord, inserted in the extremity
of the bone, forming the heel or os calcis. These,
however, would be insufficient, without a surface or
base on which the trunk itself could rest; and we
find this supplied by a broad and capacious pelvis,
with which the thigh-bones form a right angle, by
means of the length of the *cervix femoris*, or neck

of the thigh-bone. In the orangs, on the contrary, and indeed in all the monkeys, the lower extremities are comparatively short, while the upper, or arms, are very long, so as to allow the knuckles to be applied to the ground when the animal is nearly erect, and which is, in fact, the mode of progression always adopted when necessity requires this position. The black orang noticed by Dr Tyson advanced in this manner, and that dissected by Dr Trail was observed never to place " the palms of the hands on the ground." Dr Abel's red orang performed " the progressive motion by placing his bent fists upon the ground, and drawing his body between his arms." The narrowness of the pelvis, and the short neck of the femur, forming an acute angle with the spine, also renders the erect position impossible for any time, and always irksome, which is farther confirmed by the weakness of the muscles. The glutei are scarcely visible, and the calves are very weak.*

The *extensors* of the knee are much stronger in the human subject than in other mammalia, as their operation of extending the thigh forwards on the leg, forms a very essential part in the human mode o progression. The *flexors* of the knee are, on the contrary, stronger in animals, and are inserted so much lower down, even in the monkeys, that the cord which they form keeps the knee habitually bent,

* " Les fesses étoient presque nulles, ainsi que les mollets "— F. CUVIER.

F

and almost prevents the perfect extension of the leg
on the thigh.* " The motion of the knee-joint in the
black orang was free backwards, but the animal does
not seem capable of perfect extension of this joint, from
the contraction of the posterior muscles of the limb." †

Continuing the organization of the lower extremity,
we shall now examine the foot. In man, the whole
surface of the tarsus, metatarsus, and toes, rests upon
the ground, and the os calcis forms a right angle with
the leg. In the orangs, this bone begins to form an
acute angle with the limb, and consequently does not
rest upon the ground. The sole of the foot becomes
narrower ; and in all the attempts at erect progression,
exhibited by the orangs which have been shown in

* Dr Trail.

† " The most remarkable muscle about the top of the thigh, has
not been noticed by Tyson, Camper, Cuvier, or the older anato-
mists. It is a flat triangular muscle, arising from the whole anterior
edge of the ileum to within half an inch of the acetabulum, and is
inserted just below the fore part of the great trochanter, between
the head of the cruralis and vastus externus, a little below the
origin of the former. It is thin and fleshy through its whole
extent, except where it is inserted by a very short flattened tendon.
At its upper part it is united by cellular substance to the iliacus
internus. The action of this muscle appears to be intended to
assist in climbing. On this account, we propose to name it the
scandens, or musculus scansorius ; and we are disposed to regard
it as one of the principal peculiarities in *Simia satyrus.*"—Dr
Trail. *Account of Black Orang*. Wern. Soc. Trans. Vol.
iii. p. 29.

this country, the foot was observed to rest on its outer edge. The plantaris muscle also, which is very fleshy among quadrumanous animals, instead of terminating, as it does in man, by insertion in the os calcis, passes over that bone into the sole, and is there connected with the plantar aponeurosis, an arrangement incompatible with the erect attitude, as the tendon would be compressed, and its action impeded, if the heel rested on the ground.* But the most marked peculiarity in the foot, and one which is instantly perceived, is the great length of the phalanges or toes, and the position of the great toe, which is placed nearly in a line with the ankle, and does not reach, at the nail, within an inch of the first metatarsal joint, having the appearance of a thumb and hand, whose office it in reality performs. Nor is the internal conformation less remarkable; the whole arrangement of muscles is much nearer to that of a hand; but the thumbs of both the fore and hind extremities have no separate flexor longus, (long flexor,) but receive tendons from the flexors of the fingers. "Hence, the thumbs in these animals will generally be bent together with the other fingers; and they are less capable of those actions in which the motion of the thumb is combined with that of the fore and middle finger—a combination so important in numerous delicate operations."†

The upper extremity approaches much nearer to the

* Lawrence, Nat. Hist. of Man. † Ibid. page 162.

human form, and in its similarity points out the
unfitness of these animals for a constant quadruped
motion.   The inferior structure of the hands, and
particularly the thumbs, show them fitted for grasping
alone, and incapable of performing any nice mecha-
nical operation, while the great comparative length
indicates their utility in climbing, and therefore their
fitness for an arboreal life.

All the orangs which have been dissected, had
scarcely reached their second year. The relative proportions, therefore, of the skull and brain to the body,
cannot be fixed or compared with those of the adult
human being. The relations of the brain, however,
as far as have been observed, are nearly similar, and
the principal differences in the skull of the nearest
form, the black orang, are thus mentioned by Dr Trail:
" The top of the head is more flat, and its union
with the spine farther back. The orbital processes of
the os frontis project about half an inch beyond the
general convexity of that bone ; and the orbits of the
eyes are proportionally larger and rounder than in
man. The depression which receives the cribriform
plate of the ethmoid bone, is much deeper and smoother
on the sides; while the apertures in that bone, for
the passage of the olfactory nerves, are considerably
larger. Instead of the well-defined boundaries traced
in the human skull by the crucial ridge, they were
marked by a flat undulation of the occipital bone.
There is no mastoid, and scarcely a vestige of a hyloid

process, (consequently the muscles which arise from these processes in man, have a different origin.) The bones of the nose were placed perfectly flat on the face, so as not to be visible in the profile of the skull, and the triangular opening was circular. The supramaxillary bones projected considerably beyond the remarkable orbiter process of the frontal bone, being the form of the lower part of the bone nearer to that of quadrupeds. The lower jaw was stronger and narrower."

The superior maxillary bones in man are united to each other, and contain the whole of the upper teeth ; but in most of the mammaliæ, they are separated by a third bone of a wedge shape, which contains the incisor teeth. Blumenbach named this the *os inter-maxillare.* According to that anatomist, and Camper, it is found in the red orang; whereas, according to Tyson and Daubenton, it was not seen in the chimpanzee, or black orang; nor does Dr Trail mention having observed it in the specimen which he dissected. " The brute face," says Lawrence, " is merely an instrument, adapted to procure and prepare food, and often a weapon of offence and defence. The human countenance is an organ of expression, an outward index of what passes in the busy world within. In the animal, the elongated and narrow jaws with their muscles, with their sharp cutting teeth, or strong-pointed and formidable fangs, compose the face ; the chin, lips, cheeks, eyebrows and forehead, are either

removed, or reduced to a size and form simply necessary for animal purposes; the nose is confounded with
the upper jaw and lip, or, if more developed, is still
applied to offices connected with procuring food." In
the whole we have the muzzle, or snout of an animal,
not the countenance of a human being.

The articulation of the head with the spine, which
determines its support, is, in the human subject, very
nearly in the centre; and the vertical line of the
neck and trunk is nearly perpendicular, and would
pass through the top of the head; consequently the
whole weight is sustained by the vertebral column.
In most animals, the great occipital hole, and the
articular condyles, are placed almost at the end of
the skull, throwing the whole weight of the head forwards, and it is incapable of being supported by the
vertebral column, without some very powerful assisting machinery. Hence, we find the spinous processes
of the cervical vertebræ long, and assisted by a
very strong ligament, called the ligamentum nuchæ,
or suspensorium colli. In the orang, the occipital
hole is placed twice as far from the jaws as from
the back of the head, which throws a great additional
weight forwards, and consequently requires more exertion to maintain the erect position. But although we
find, according to Camper, that the spinous processes
of the cervical vertebræ are long, and see a greater
developement of them in the Batavian pongo, there is
no mention in any author of the presence of the sus-

pensory ligament, which is also used as an argument
tnat the natural gait of these animals is not quadruped;
for the immense weight of the jaws of the adults, placed
so far off the centre, could not possibly be supported in
that position, without some provision of this kind.
Additional confirmation of this argument is the absence
of the suspensorium oculi, a muscle found in quadrupeds,
and evidently intended to relieve the others, and be a
greater support to the eyes when continued in the
prone position.

These are the principal peculiarities of structure connected with progression and attitude; and it must be
at once perceived, that neither the erect or quadruped
posture, is the common and natural one of the monkeys,
and that they will employ either as occasion requires,
in their silvan or rocky abodes. Every other part
of the form will present some difference; but with
the exception of the construction of the larynx, and
principal organs employed in the faculty of speech, we
shall merely mention a few of the remaining most prominent peculiarities exhibited by the African and
Asiatic orangs.

There were only four lumbar vertebræ in Dr Trail's
orang, in this respect similar to the Asiatic species dissected by Messrs Owen and Yarrel. In the first animal,
however, there were thirteen dorsal vertebræ, and a
similar number of ribs; in the latter, only twelve of
each. The lower opening of the pelvis in the black
orang is very large; the sacrum is very narrow. No

occipito-frontalis muscle was found in the black orang,
while it was distinctly seen in the red species by Messrs
Owen and Yarrel. In the same animal, three muscles
were found to supply the place of the pectoralis major;
and the peculiar muscle called the *levator claviculæ*
is found in both. In the black orang the size of the
olfactory nerve is great, and the surface of the turbi-
nated bones extensive, which would lead us to infer
that the sense of smelling was powerful, and of course
of necessary use in its economy.

The larynx of these animals present some curious
peculiarities. The best account, perhaps, is that given
by Camper of the red orang. After examining the
tongue, that anatomist continues. " pursuing my dis.
section, I discovered a large sack on the right side, run
ing over the clavicular bones, and another on the left
side, but visibly smaller. The large sack tore a little
on account of its being tender, by having lain so long
in spirits. I inflated it through the opening, which I
continued quickly, as I perceived that the air went off
betwixt the tongue bone and the thyroideus cartilage.
I then followed up the rent with a pair of scissors,
and cut open the sack, by which means I discovered a
transverse split. There was now no doubt but that
the left sack had a similar orifice.

" In pursuance of it, I took away the whole soft
palate and œsophagus as far as below the speaking
organs. The soft palate is the same as in most quadrupeds, with this difference, nevertheless, that the

uvula on the hind side runs very evidently downwards, but not beneath the margin of the soft palate. This palate appears, however, more capable than in other animals of being contracted."

In other two orangs " there was merely one single sack, having two air tubes, which united themselves with the two splits." This, he thinks, had been formerly two, " but that the two sacks were gone over into one."

In one of the animals, " the bottom (of the sack) rose nearly to the end of the breast bone, and was partly covered by the breast muscles ; the sack rose upwards above the clavicular bones, and with the appendages still more backward, so that this sack penetrated on each side deep under the monk's-hood muscles, as far as behind upon the shoulder blades."

Camper is of opinion, that this sack increases in size with the age of the animal ; and that the frequent expansion by the air, is the cause of the increase.

" The orang can, in the mean time, voluntarily swell up these sacks, or this united sack, whenever it tries or attempts to press the strongly inhaled air outwards, and presses then the epiglottis towards the openings of the larynx, or bends it only a little. It can also empty them at pleasure by means of the broad muscles of the neck, by those of the breast, and by the cuculares, or monk's-hood muscles."

In the black orang, according to Dr Trail, the os hyoides differed from that of man, in being anteriorly

more prominent and dilated, and by containing in its
body a cavity capable of holding a large pea.   On laying open the posterior part of the larynx, the two
apertures at the base of the epiglottis, and leading to
the laryngeal pouches discovered by Camper, were
visible.

The great difference in these organs from the human
are the large sacks, which evidently produce the powerful and deep sounds uttered by so many of this
tribe.   In the black orang, being carried into the body
of the os hyoides, it shows the first indication of structure so peculiarly belonging to the American howlers.
In the Siamang, remarkable for the power of voice,
the simple sacks are so extensive as to protrude pro-
minently to outward view.   They prevent the ut-
terance of systematic sounds which the other organs
might produce, by preventing a power of control over
the air.   " Every time that the animal would uttei
his cry, these sacks swell, then empty themselves, so
that he is not able, at will, to supply to the differert
parts of his mouth the sounds they might articulate.*

In intellect we consider the quadrumanous animals,
notwithstanding what has been written and recorded
of many of them, not superior, and in many cases
inferior, to others of the animal creation; it has the
same constitutional distinctions, and presents the
same great differences, from a true reasoning power.

* Richerand, Physiology, p. 424.

But among the many anecdotes related of the understanding of the orang-outang, and other monkeys, some
may be classed as under the influence of a higher power
of discrimination than mere instinct, and where a process, as it were, of discussion passed in the sensorium of
the animal. As an example of what we mean, we may
mention an anecdote of the young red orang, lately
exhibited in Edinburgh by Mr Cops, and figured on
our second plate.

Mr Cops one day gave him the half of an orange,
a fruit of which he was passionately fond, and
laid the other half aside upon the upper shelf of a
press out of his reach and sight. Some time after,
Mr Cops being reclining upon a sofa with his eyes
closed, the orang began to prowl about the room,
and showed that, notwithstanding his apparent in-
attention, the position of his favourite orange had
been narrowly watched. Anxious to see the result,
he continued quiet, and feigned sleep. Jocko
cautiously approached the sofa, examined as far
as he could that his guardian was sound, and mount-
ing quietly and expeditiously, finished the remaining
half of the orange, carefully concealed the peel in the
grate among some paper shavings, and having again
examined Mr Cops, and seeing nothing doubtful in
the reality of his sleep, retired confidently to his own
couch. Here there must have been a detailed series
of impressions during the progress of the action ;
but in common with the construction of the brute

mind, he was incapable of extending the power farther, or of *reasoning* upon that action, during the performance of which his intellect had gone through several distinct processes. All their actions in a state of confinement may be traced to the same source, while those in a state of nature will be more akin to instinct, and will be performed under the impulses of the various passions.

Cunning joined with caution, an inquisitive and prying turn, and imitativeness, are the strong characters in the disposition of the whole family. All these faculties and propensities become more developed in a state of confinement, and consequently of tuition, than in their natural wildness ; and while the first, in both states, is indispensable for their preservation, it is by the influence of the others that they are principally indebted to confinement, and the parts they are made to perform in the beggarly dramas performed in the streets of our great towns. Their power of imitation is very great, and often ludicrous in the extreme, from the expressive face, and human-like form of the upper parts. This *talent* has even been said to have been used to their own destruction ;—we have heard of monkeys cutting their throats, in imitation of the feigned action of the person whom they annoyed, and of one who killed himself by infusing a paper of tobacco with milk and sugar, instead of tea, and drinking it as he had observed some sick sailor do. How far these are true we shall not attempt to decide ;

certain it is, that these animals most ludicrously possess this propensity, and that those we have seen as
pets, would almost perform any thing once pointed out
to them, and would always make the attempt.

For the arrangement of these animals in the de-
scriptive part of our volume, we have followed the old
practice of dividing them into two great geographical
groups, while we have introduced most of the new
genera. This plan we found to be the most convenient
during the progress, and perhaps liable to less objec-
tion in a work of this kind, than any other or newer
system, all of which yet fall short of our own ideas
of their correct classification.

The truest arrangement that has yet been proposed,
is that by Cuvier and Geoffroy Saint Hilaire,* and
they place the Sapajous immediately after the Orangs
and Gibbons. Another system of arrangement, which
would find both its friends and enemies in the ad-
vocates and disparagers of the circular or progressive series, would be to descend from the Orangs, on the
one side of the circle, by the Gibbons, Nasalis, and
Colobus, the latter being the only form in the old
world with four fingers to the upper extremities, and
so far in this respect representing the genus *Ateles*
of the new. We have then the genus *Lasiopyga*,
which combines a great flatness of face to the form of
the Guenons which naturally follow. and thence the

* Journal de Physique.

passage to the Baboons and *Cynocephali* is easy. On the opposite side, we would descend by the Sapajous and Sagoins to *Ateles*, thence to the Howlers or Baboons of the new world, and onwards by the *Pithecia* or Desmarets, to the small species with hooked and sharp claws. We would still, in this way, have a space between these diminutive insectivorous species, deviating so much from the *quadrumanous* type and the *cynocephalous* baboons; but this appears to fill itself naturally up by the *Lemuridæ*, the small species of which seem intimately connected with the little monkeys above mentioned, while there will be a natural gradation from the baboons to the genus *Licha-notus* of Illiger, or the *Indri* of Sonnerat and Audibert. This view of their arrangement would doubtless re-- quire alterations to perfect it; but something of the kind seems the most natural method, and the orders of the Carnivora and Rodentia, whichever shall be found to follow most naturally, would touch at the various points of the circle representing their respec- tive families.

For the illustrations of the present volume, we have been at considerable pains. In a few instances Mr Lizars has been able to draw from the living animals, and our best thanks are due to Mr Cops, for allowing copies to be made from his interesting specimen of the red orang, and also to Mr Wombwell for the sketch of the white eyelid monkey. Professor Jameson pointed out the specimen of the hoolack lately re-

ceived in the Edinburgh Museum; and for the re-
mainder we are indebted to the beautiful but expen-
sive works of the continental naturalists. We have
made free use of Humboldt's Zoological Observations, and his History of the Monkeys of the Ori-
nooko; of Frederic Cuvier's great work on the Mammaliæ; Audibert, Histoire Naturelle des Singes, and
of Spix and Martius's History of the New Brazilian
species.

Having thus so far endeavoured to detail the habits
and economy of this curious family, and the general
plan of our volume, we shall at once proceed to the
description of the animals themselves.

MONKEYS OF ASIA AND AFRICA, OR THOSE OF THE OLD WORLD.

THE ORANGS.

THE animals which have generally been placed in this division are those, which of all creation, approach nearest to man in their structure. They have generally been placed first in our systems, and we have now to point out those characters important in arrangement, and the distinctions which will separate the species. They have been divided into three genera, the first of which is named *Troglodytes* by Geoffroy Saint Hilaire, and is characterised by a facial angle of 50°; distinct superciliary ridges; the canine teeth slightly elongated, and placed close to the cutting teeth, as in man; the head rounded; the muzzle short; no tail, cheek pouches, or callosities; the ears resembling those of man, but large and projecting. It contains only one species.

Stewart delt.   Lizars sc.

TROGLODYTES NIGER.

(The Black Orang.)

THE BLACK ORANG.

Troglodytes niger.—Geoffroy.

Plate I.

Great Ape, *Pennant.*—Troglodytes chimpanzee, *Geoffroy Saint Hilaire, Annales du Museum,* xix. p. 87.—Troglodytes niger, *Desmarets Mammalogie,* page 49.—Black Orang of Africa, *Illustrations of Zoology by James Wilson,* plate v. fig. 2.—*Dr Trail, Transactions of Wernerian Society,* vol. iii. p. 1.

This singular animal has been mentioned by various travellers under the names of Baris, Smitten, Quimpere, and Quojas-moras; but the adult state remains in even greater obscurity than that of its Asiatic representative, which we shall next endeavour to describe. The relations of all travellers agree in the large and powerful stature which this animal attains, and we have every reason to believe that this is the fact, though they are always so mixed up with the marvellous, and with accounts of their habits and sagacity, so different from the attributes of an animal, that we must certainly consider them undecided without some more direct testimony; and, from their apparent incorrectness, the other parts of the relations have always been received with a doubt.

The black orang is a native of Africa, and particularly the Guinea Coast and Angola; they are said to live in vast troops, and to be dangerous in their attacks upon persons travelling alone in the forests where they are found. They are covered with shining black hair, longest on the back and shoulders; our description of the adult state is, however, imperfect, and we refer to the minute detail given by Dr Trail of a young specimen. Previous to mentioning it, we may relate an account from Bingley's Animal Biography of a large specimen of this creature, which seems to have been given upon some better authority than most of the others :—" Allemand, the Dutch professor of natural history, had received many vague and unsatisfactory accounts respecting an animal of this kind, and was induced to write to Mr May, a captain in the Dutch naval service stationed at Surinam. This gentleman found him exactly similar to one which he had brought from Guinea, except in size. He was nearly five feet and a half high, and very strong and powerful. Mr May had seen him take up his master, a stout man, by the middle, and fling him from him for a pace or two; and one day he seized a soldier, who happened to pass carelessly near the tree to which he was chained, and, if his master had not been present, he would actually have carried the man into the tree."

The age of this animal, when Mr May first saw it, was about twenty-one years. It died in the following year, but had evidently increased in height during the interval. If we may depend on this account, we may thence conclude that the height will reach six feet at least, while the age attained by them will naturally be considerable.

Young animals have only been exhibited in this country, and we shall now give the account of Dr Trail of one shown in Liverpool. We have extracted it from the Transactions of the Wernerian Society :—

" It was a female, and was procured in the Isle of Princes in the Gulf of Guinea, from a native trader, who had carried it thither from the banks of the Gaboon. It was represented as a young animal, far inferior in size to the specimens often seen in the recesses of its native forests; and Captain Payne observed, that it was at least eight or ten inches lower in stature than another which he had seen in the Isle of Princes.

" The natives of Gaboon informed him, that this species attains the height of five or six feet, that it is a formidable antagonist to the elephant, and that several of them will not scruple to attack the lion, and other beasts of prey, with clubs and stones. It is dangerous for solitary individuals to travel through the woods haunted by the orang outang ; and instances were related to Captain Payne of negro girls being carried of by this animal, who have sometimes escaped to human society, after having been for years detain by their ravishers in a frightful captivity. These reports confirm the narratives of the early voyagers, who have often been suspected of exaggeration, and similar facts have been recently stated, very circumstantially, by gentlemen who have lived in Western Africa.

' When first our animal came on board,' says Captain Payne, ' it shook hands with some of the sailors, but refused its hand, with marks of anger, to others, without any apparent cause. It speedily, however, became familiar with the crew, except one boy, to whom it never was reconciled. When the seamen's mess was brought on deck, it was a constant attendant ; would go round and embrace each person, while it uttered loud yells, and then seat itself among them to share the repast.' When angry, it sometimes made a barking noise like a dog ; at other times it would cry like a pettish child, and scratch itself with great vehemence. It expressed satisfaction, especially on receiving sweetmeats, ' by a sound like *hem*, in a grave tone ;' but it seems to have little variety in its voice. In warm latitudes, it was active and cheerful, but became languid as it receded from the torrid zone ; and on approaching our shores, it showed a desire to have a warm covering, and would roll itself carefully up in a blanket when it retired to rest. It generally walked on all fours ; and Captain Payne particularly remarked, that it never placed the palm of the hands of its fore extremities to the ground, but, closing its fists, rested on the knuckles ; a circumstance also noticed by Tyson, which was confirmed to me by a young navy officer, who had been for a considerable time employed in the rivers of Western Africa, and had opportunities of observing the habits of this species. This animal did not seem fond of the erect posture, which it rarely affected, though it could run nimbly on two feet for a short distance. In this case, it appeared to aid the motion of its legs by grasping the thighs with its hands. It had great strength in the four fingers of its superior extremity; for it would often swing by them on a rope upwards of an hour, without intermission. When first procured, it was so thickly covered with hair that the skin of the trunk and limbs was scarcely visible, until the long black hair was blown aside. It ate readily every sort of vegetable food; but at first did not appear to relish flesh, though it seemed to have pleasure in sucking the leg-bone of a fowl. At that time it did not relish wine, but afterwards seemed to like it, though it never could endure ardent spirits. It once stole a bottle of wine, which it uncorked with its teeth, and began to drink. It showed a predilection for coffee; and was immoderately fond of sweet articles of food. It learned to feed itself with a spoon, to drink out of a glass, and showed a general disposition to imitate the actions of men. It was attracted by bright metals, seemed to take pride in clothing, and often put a cocked hat on its head. It was dirty in its habits, and never was known to wash itself. It was afraid of fire-arms ; and, on the whole, appeared a timid animal.

" It lived with Captain Payne seventeen weeks, two of which were spent in Cork and Liverpool. At the former place it was exhibited for the benefit of the soup kitchen for a few days, but seems to have been there neglected. On coming to Liverpool, it languish- ed a few days, moaned heavily, was oppressed in its breathing, and died with convulsive motions of the limbs.

" When erect this animal is about thirty inches high. The skin appears of a yellowish-white colour, and is thinly covered with long black hair on the front ; but it is considerably more hairy behind. The hair on the head is rather thin, and is thickest on the forehead, where it divides about an inch above the orbiter pro- cess of the frontal bone, and, running a little back- wards, falls down before the ears, forming whiskers on the cheeks. Here the hair measures nearly two inches long ; but that on the occiput is not above an inch in length. There are a few stiff black hairs on the eye- brows, and a scanty eyelash. A few whitish hairs are scattered on the lips, especially on the under one. The rest of the face is naked, and has whitish and wrinkled skin. There is scarcely any hair on the neck ; but, commencing at the nape, it becomes somewhat bushy on the back. The abdomen is nearly naked. The hair on the back of the head, and the whole trunk,

front of the lower extremities, back of the legs, and
upper part of the superior extremities, is directed
downwards, while that on the back of the thigh and
fore arms is pointed upwards; appearances well represented in Tyson's figure. The longest hair is just at the
elbows. There is none on the fingers or palms of either
extremity. The ears are remarkably prominent, thin,
and naked, bearing a considerable resemblance in shape
to the human, though broader at the top. The projection of the process above the eyes is very conspicuous, but has not been sufficiently marked in any
engraving or drawing which has fallen under my observation. The nose is quite flat, or rather appears
only as a wrinkle of the skin, with a slight depression
along its centre. The nostrils are patulous, and open
upwards, which would be inconvenient did the animal usually assume the erect posture. The projection
of the jaws is excessive, and though much less so than
in the babbon, yet the profile of the face is concave.
It may be remarked, however, that the projection of
the lower jaw is caricatured in the first and second
figures of Camper's second plate. The mouth is wide,
the lips rather thin, and destitute of that recurvation
of the edges which add so much to the expression of
the human countenance. The whole contour of the
head bears no inconsiderable resemblance to some
Egyptian figures of the god Anubis.

" The spread of the shoulders is distinctly marked,
but the width of the lower part of the chest is propor

tionally greater, when compared to the upper, than in
man.

" From the lower ribs, the diameter of the abdomen
decreases rapidly to the loins, where the animal is
peculiarly slender; a circumstance in which it approaches the other *Simiæ*. The pelvis appears long
and narrow, another approximation to the rest of the
genus.

" With regard to the limbs, the chief difference
between our specimen and Dr Tyson's figure, consists
in the excessive length of the arms, which in this
animal descend below the knees, by the whole length
of the phalanges of the fingers, which are above three
inches in length. The same observation applies to
almost every figure of this animal which I have seen.
The proportions in the work of Camper approach
nearest, in the present instance, in this particular.
The hand differs from the human, in having the
thumb by far the smallest of the fingers. The foot is
more properly a hand appended to a tarsus. The
thumb of this extremity is very long, powerful, and
capable of great extension. The legs are certainly
furnished with calves; but they scarcely resemble the
human in form, because they are continued of equal
thickness nearly to the heel. When this animal is
erect, the knees appear considerably bent, as is the case
with the other *Simiæ*, and it stands with the limbs
more apart than man."

Such is the minute description by Dr Trail. Another specimen of this animal, and one of the Asiatic

species, were exhibited together in the Egyptian Hall, Piccadilly, in 1831, and afforded a treat to the lovers of zoology. They were both very young; the black orang had been procured by a trading vessel on the river Gambia, and was much the most pleasing of the two. He was compared to a black child, but with a head of overgrown proportions. He was very docile, and generally playful and gentle; like all his tribe, he was fond of wine and water, or diluted spirits; and they were used as an incentive for him to perform his part before strangers. Neither of these animals survived long, but fell victims to cold, which seems invariably to affect the orangs, generally before the expiry of the first winter.

Our plate is taken from a stuffed specimen in the Edinburgh Museum, which, though not in a very good or entire state of preservation, agrees generally with the above descriptions.

The second form among the orangs is described by Geoffroy under the title of *Pithecus*. The young state of this animal may be said to be well known, and at an age of from three to five years, may be characterized by a facial angle of 65°; by the canine teeth exceeding the others in length,* and the molar teeth being nearly square on the upper surface; the head rounded, no cheek pouches or callosities;

* In the adult, the canine teeth will far exceed the others in length. as much nearly as among the strong carnivora.

the ears resembling those of man, but small, and applied close to the head; the arms of considerable length. In the adult state, from what we imperfectly know, these characters will vary widely, and still more so if the *Pongo* shall ultimately prove identical with it, which the high authority of Cuvier would now warrant us to consider decided, did there not exist so very wide a difference between the characters given by him and Lacépède, and those which so many in the young state have exhibited. We have added the dentition of the Pongo from Frederic Cuvier, reduced two-thirds, and the resemblance between it and the teeth of the large Sumatran orang, will be immediately seen.

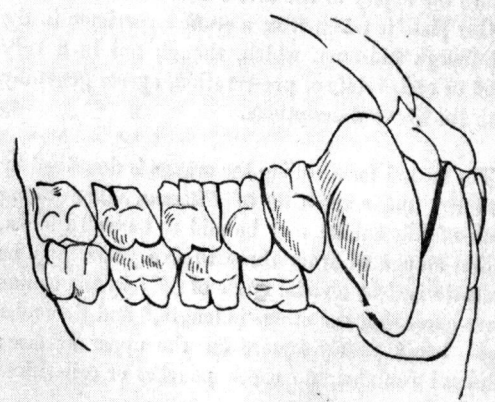

PLATE 2

PITHECUS SATYRUS.

[The Red or Asiatic Orang-outang]

PLATE 2*

Stewart del.   Lizars sc.

PITHECUS SATYRUS.
(The Red or Asiatic Orang-outang.)

THE RED OR ASIATIC ORANG-OUTANG.

Pithecus satyrus.— GEOFFROY.

PLATES II. and II*.

Simia satyrus, *Linnæus.*—Jocko, *Audibert, Histoire Naturelle des Singes.* —Pithecus satyrus, *Desmarets Mammologie,* p. 50; *Geoffroy Saint Hilaire, Annales du Museum,* xix. p. 88.—The Red or Asiatic Orang-Outang, *James Wilson's Illustrations of Zoology,* pl. v. figs. 1 and 3.—Orang-Outang, *Abel, Embassy to China,* pages 319 and 365.

WE are fortunately possessed of more ample materials to illustrate the history of this singular animal, than of the black orang of Africa; but it is to be regretted that what we have, also relate to individuals in a comparatively young state. One instance only of the capture of what may be considered an adult specimen is authentically recorded; and the fragments of that specimen, with the skull of a supposed adult in the collection at Paris, are all from which we can draw the true characters of this creature. Of the existence of a most gigantic animal there can be no doubt; but it must either be an inhabitant of the interior only, or must flee most rapidly from the encroachments of civilization. The first is the most probable; for it is scarcely possible, if ever an inhabitant of the coasts, that a solitary individual only should have been observed, during the very long period that this country has been possessed by Europeans, among whom were men most zealous in the pursuit of natural history, and to whom this had been long held up as one of the greatest acquisitions that could be procured. This will appear the less singular when we consider the immense extent of unknown territory, occupied by forests almost boundless, and of the most impenetrable description, and we may easily conceive that they will possess many tenants, hitherto unseen even to the piercing eyes of their native hunters. The most unaccountable circumstance is, that the young are so frequently met with, while the gigantic parents have scarcely been perceived; and, except in the instance we have mentioned, exist only in the accounts handed down from family to family.

We have seen the black orang of Africa to be very local in the extent of its distribution, inhabiting but a small portion of a vast continent. The red orang possesses the same peculiarity in its range, and seems confined to the Islands of Borneo and Sumatra, and to the peninsula of Malacca, inhabiting the immense forests, and rarely appearing on their outskirts.

Since the arrival, in 1818, of the red orang, figured and so admirably described by Dr Abel, several young specimens have been exhibited in England, and notes of their manners while alive, with accounts of their dissections, have generally been made and published. None of these are equal, however, in minuteness or interest to that of the assiduous naturalist we have now mentioned; and though it has been frequently copied into works treating of this subject, and is very generally known, we should not consider the present description complete without it. Dr Abel had a long opportunity of observing the animal, and under less constraint than any of those which have since reached Britain. He was interested in, and well qualified for the task, and his whole account bears the stamp of truth, and close unbiased observation. We give the description in his words, and unabridged.*

" This interesting animal was procured by Captain Methuen, who brought him from Banjarmassing, on the south coast of Borneo. He was informed by the natives that he had been brought from the highlands of the interior : that he was very rare and difficult to take ; and they evidently considered him a great curiosity, as they flocked in crowds to see him.

" The height of the animal, judging from his length

* It was from this animal that the accurate figures in Mr James Wilson's " Illustrations of Zoology" were taken. The drawings were made by the celebrated Howit, and were furnished to the author by Dr Trail, Professor of Medical Jurisprudence in the Edinburgh University.

when laid on a flat surface, and measured from his heel to the crown of his head, is two feet seven inches. The hair is of a brownish-red colour, and covers his back, arms, legs, and outside of his hands and feet. On the back it is in some places six inches long, and on his arms five. It is thinly scattered over the back of his hands and feet, and is very short. It is directed downwards on the back, upper arm, and legs, and up-wards on the fore arm. It is directed from behind forwards on the head, and inwards on the inside of the thighs. The face has no hair, except on its sides, somewhat in the manner of whiskers, and a very thin beard. The middle of the breast and belly was naked on his arrival in England, but has since become hairy. The shoulders, elbows, and knees, have fewer hairs than other parts of the arms and legs. The palms of the hands and feet are quite naked.

" The prevailing colour of the animal's skin, when naked, or seen through the hair, is a bluish-grey. The eyelids and margin of the mouth are of a light copper colour. The inside of his hands and feet are of a deep copper colour. Two copper-coloured stripes pass from the armpits down each side of the body, as low as the navel.

" The head viewed in front, is pear-shaped, expand-ing from the chin upwards, the cranium being much the larger end. The eyes are close together, of an oval form, and dark brown colour. The eyelids are fringed with lashes, and the lower ones are saccular and wrinkled. The nose is confluent with the face, except at the nostrils, which are but little elevated; their openings are narrow and oblique. The mouth is very projecting, and of a roundish mammillary form. Its opening is large, but when closed is marked by little more than a narrow seam. The lips are very narrow, and scarcely perceptible when the mouth is shut. The chin projects less than the mouth; below it, a pendulous membrane gives the appearance of a double chin, and swells out when the animal is angry or much pleased. Each of the jaws contains twelve teeth, namely, four incisive teeth, the two middle ones of the upper jaw being twice the width of the lateral; two canine, and six double teeth. The ears are small, closely resemble the human ear, and have their lower margins in the same line with the external angles of the eyes.

" The chest is wide compared with the pelvis; the belly is very protuberant. The arms are long in proportion to the height of the animal, their span measuring full four feet seven inches and a half. The legs are short compared with the arms.

" The hands are long, compared with their width, and with the human hand. The fingers are small and tapering; the thumb is very short, scarcely reaching the first joint of the forefinger. All the fingers have very perfect nails, of a blackish colour and oval form, and exactly terminating with the extremities of the fingers. The feet are long, resemble hands in the palms, and in having fingers rather than toes, but have heels resembling the human. The great toes are very short, are set on at right angles to the feet close to the heel, and are entirely without nails.

" The orang-outang of Borneo is utterly incapable of walking in a perfectly erect posture. He betrays this in his whole exterior conformation, and never wilfully attempts to counteract its tendency. His head leaning forward, and forming a considerable angle with the back, throws the centre of gravity so far beyond the perpendicular, that his arms, like the forelegs of other animals, are required to support the body. So difficult indeed is it for him to keep the upright position for a few seconds, under the direction of his keeper, that he is obliged, in the performance of his task, to raise his arms above his head, and throw them behind him to keep his balance. His progressive motion on a flat surface is accomplished by placing his bent fists upon the ground, and drawing his body between his arms ; moving in this manner, he strongly resembles a person decrepid in the legs, supported on stilts. In a state of nature, he probably seldom moves along the ground ; his whole external configuration showing his fitness for climbing trees and clinging to their branches. The length and pliability of his fingers and toes enable him to grasp with facility and steadiness ; and the force of his muscles empowers him to support his body for a great length of time by one hand or foot. He can thus pass from one fixed object to another, at the distance of his span from each other, and can obviously pass from one branch of a tree to another, through a much greater interval. In sitting on a flat surface, this animal turns his legs under him. In sitting on the branch of a tree, or on a rope, he rests on his heels, his body leaning forward against his thighs. This animal uses his hands like others of the monkey tribe.

" The orang-outang, on his arrival in Java from Batavia, was allowed to be entirely at liberty till within a day or two of being put on board the Cæsar, to be conveyed to England; and whilst at large, made no attempt to escape, but became violent when put into a large railed bamboo cage for the purpose of being conveyed from the island. As soon as he felt himself in confinement, he took the rails of the cage into his hands, and shaking them violently, endeavoured to break them in pieces; but finding that they did not yield generally, he tried them separately, and having discovered one weaker than the rest, worked at it constantly till he had broken it, and made his escape. On board ship, an attempt being made to secure him by a chain tied to a strong staple, he instantly unfastened it, and ran off with the chain dragging behind; but finding himself embarrassed by its length, he coiled it once or twice, and threw it over his shoulder. This feat he often repeated, and when he found that it would not remain on his shoulder, he took it into his mouth.

"After several abortive attempts to secure him more effectually, he was allowed to wander freely about the ship, and soon became familiar with the sailors, and surpassed them in agility.

"They often chased him about the rigging, and gave him frequent opportunities of displaying his adroitness in managing an escape. On first starting, he would endeavour to outstrip his pursuers by mere speed, but when much pressed, elude them by seizing a loose rope, and swinging out of their reach. At other times he would patiently wait on the shrouds, or at the mast-head, till his pursuers almost touched him, and then suddenly lower himself to the deck by any rope that was near him, or bound along the mainstay from one mast to the other, swinging by his hands, and moving them one over the other. The men would often shake the ropes by which he clung with so much violence, as to make me fear his falling, but I soon found that the power of his muscles could not be easily overcome. When in a playful humour, he would often swing within arms-length of his pursuer, and having struck him with his hand, throw himself from him.

"Whilst in Java, he lodged in a large tamarind tree near my dwelling, and formed a bed by intertwining the small branches and covering them with leaves. During the day, he would lie with his head projecting

beyond his nest, watching whoever might pass under,
and when he saw any one with fruit, would descend
to obtain a share of it. He always retired for the
night at sunset, or sooner if he had been well fed; and
rose with the sun, and visited those from whom he
habitually received food.

" On board ship, he commonly slept at the mast-
head, after wrapping himself in a sail. In making
his bed, he used the greatest pains to remove every
thing out of his way that might render the surface on
which he intended to lie uneven ; and having satisfied
himself with this part of his arrangement, spread out
the sail, and lying down upon it on his back, drew it
over his body. Sometimes I preoccupied his bed, and
teased him by refusing to give it up. On these occasions he would endeavour to pull the sail from under
me, or to force me from it, and would not rest till I
had resigned it ; if it was large enough for both, he
would quietly lie by my side. If all the sails happened to be set, he would hunt about for some other
covering, and either steal one of the sailors' jackets or
shirts that happened to be drying, or empty a hammock of its blankets. Off the Cape of Good Hope,
he suffered much from a low temperature, especially
early in the morning, when he would descend from
the mast, shuddering with cold, and running up to
any one of his friends, climb into their arms, and
clasping them closely, derive warmth from their

persons, screaming violently at any attempt to remove him.

" His food in Java was chiefly fruit, especially man-
gostans, of which he was excessively fond. He also
sucked eggs with voracity, and often employed himself in seeking them. On board ship, his diet was
of no definite kind. He ate readily of all kinds of meat,
and especially raw meat; was very fond of bread, but
always preferred fruits when he could obtain them.

" His beverage in Java was water; on board ship
it was as diversified as his food. He preferred coffee
and tea, but would readily take wine, and exemplified
his attachment to spirits, by stealing the captain's
brandy bottle. Since his arrival in London, he has
preferred beer and milk to anything else, but drinks
wine and other liquors.

" In his attempts to obtain food, he afforded us
many opportunities of judging of his sagacity and disposition. He was always very impatient to seize it
when held out to him, and became passionate when
it was not soon given up, and would chase a person
all over the ship to obtain it.   I seldom came on deck
without sweetmeats or fruit in my pocket, and could
never escape his vigilant eye. Sometimes I endeavoured to evade him by ascending to the mast-head,
but was always overtaken or intercepted in my progress. When he came up with me on the shrouds,
he would secure himself by one foot to the rattling,
and confine my legs with the other and one of his

hands, whilst he rifled my pockets. If he found it impossible to overtake me, he would climb to a considerable height on the loose rigging, and then drop suddenly upon me. Or if, perceiving his intention, I attempted to descend, he would slide down a rope and meet me at the bottom of the shrouds. Sometimes I fastened an orange to the end of a rope, and lowered it to the deck from the mast-head ; and as soon as he attempted to seize it, drew it rapidly up. After being several times foiled in endeavouring to obtain it by direct means, he altered his plan. Appearing to care little about it, he would remove to some distance, and ascend the rigging very leisurely for some time, and then, by a sudden spring, catch the rope which held it. If defeated again, by my suddenly jerking the rope, he would at first seem quite in despair, relinquish his effort, and rush about the rigging screaming violently. But he would always return, and again seizing the rope, disregard the jerk, and allow it to run through his hand till within reach of the orange ; but if again foiled, would come to my side, and taking me by the arm, confine it whilst he hauled the orange up.

" This animal neither practises the grimace and antics of other monkeys, nor possesses their perpetual proneness to mischief. Gravity approaching to melancholy and mildness, were sometimes strongly expressed in his countenance, and seem to be the characteristics of his disposition. When he first came amongst

strangers, he would sit for hours with his hand upon
his head, looking pensively at all around him; or, when
much incommoded by their examination, would hide
himself beneath any covering that was at hand. His
mildness was evinced by his forbearance under in-
juries, which were grievous before he was excited to
revenge ; but he always avoided those who often
teased him. He soon became strongly attached to
those who kindly used him. By their side he was
fond of sitting ; and, getting as close as possible to
their persons, would take their hands between his
lips, and fly to them for protection. From the boatswain of the Alceste, who shared his meals with him,
and was his chief favourite, although he sometimes
purloined the grog and the biscuit of his benefactor, he
learned to eat with a spoon ; and might be often seen
sitting at his cabin-door enjoying his coffee, quite
unembarrassed by those who observed him, and with
a grotesque and sober air that seemed a burlesque on
human nature.

" Next to the boatswain, I was perhaps his most intimate acquaintance. He would always follow me to the
mast-head, whither I often went for the sake of reading apart from the noise of the ship ; and having satisfied himself that my pockets contained no eatables,
would lie down by my side, and pulling a topsail
entirely over him, peep from it occasionally to watch
my movements.

" His favourite amusement in Java was in swing-

ing from the branches of trees, in passing from one
tree to another, and in climbing over the roofs of
houses; on board, in hanging by his arms from the
ropes, and in romping with the boys of the ship.
He would entice them into play by striking them
with his hand as they passed, and bounding from them,
but allowing them to overtake him and engage in a
mock scuffle, in which he used his hands, feet, and
mouth. If any conjecture could be formed from these
frolics of his mode of attacking an adversary, it would
appear to be his first object to throw him down, then
to secure him with his hands and feet, and then wound
him with his teeth.

" Of some small monkeys on board from Java he
took little notice, whilst under the observation of the
persons in the ship. Once, indeed, he openly attempted
to throw a small cage containing three of them over-
board; because, probably, he had seen them receive
food of which he could obtain no part. But although
he held so little intercourse with them under our in-
spection, I had reason to suspect that he was less
indifferent to their society when free from our observation, and was one day summoned to the top-gallant
yard of the mizen-mast to overlook him playing with
a young male monkey. Lying on his back, partially
covered with the sail, he for some time contemplated,
with great gravity, the gambols of the monkey which
bounded over him, but at length caught him by the

tail, and tried to envelope him in his covering. The
monkey seemed to dislike the confinement, and broke
from him, but again renewed its gambols, and although
frequently caught, always escaped. The intercourse,
however, did not seem to be that of equals, for the
orang-outang never condescended to romp with the
monkey as he did with the boys of the ship. Yet the
monkeys had evidently a great predilection for his
company; for whenever they broke loose, they took
their way to his resting-place, and were often seen
lurking about it, or creeping clandestinely towards
him. There appeared to be no gradation in their in-
timacy; as they appeared as confidently familiar with
him when first observed as at the close of their
acquaintance.

" But although so gentle when not exceedingly
irritated, the orang-outang could be excited to violent
rage, which he expressed by opening his mouth, showing
his teeth, seizing and biting those who were near him.
Sometimes, indeed, he seemed to be almost driven to
desperation; and on two or three occasions committed
an act which, in a rational being, would have been
called the threatening of suicide. If repeatedly refused an orange when he attempted to take it, he
would shriek violently and swing furiously about the
ropes; then return and endeavour to obtain it; if
again refused, he would roll for some time like an
angry child upon the deck, uttering the most piercing

screams; and then suddenly starting up, rush furiously over the side of the ship, and disappear. On first witnessing this act, we thought that he had thrown himself into the sea; but, on a search being made, found him concealed under the chains.

" I have seen him exhibit violent alarm on two occasions only, when he appeared to seek for safety in gaining as high an elevation as possible. On seeing eight large turtle brought on board, whilst the Cæsar was off the Island of Ascension, he climbed with all possible speed to a higher part of the ship than he had ever before reached; and looking down upon them, projected his long lips into the form of a hog's snout, uttering at the same time a sound which might be described as between the croaking of a frog and the grunting of a pig. After some time he ventured to descend, but with great caution, peeping continually at the turtle, but could not be induced to approach within many yards of them. He ran to the same height, and uttered the same sounds, on seeing some men bathing and splashing in the sea; and since his arrival in England, has shown nearly the same degree of fear at the sight of a live tortoise.

" Such were the actions of this animal as far as they fell under Captain Methuen's notice during his voyage from Java. I cannot find, since his arrival in England, that he has learnt to perform more than two feats which he did not practise on board ship, although his education has been by no means neglected.

One of these is to walk upright, or rather on his feet, unsupported by his hands; the other to kiss his keeper. I have before remarked with how much difficulty he accomplishes the first, and may add. that a well-trained dancing-dog would far surpass him in the imitation of the human posture."

The next specimen of which we have an accurate account, was one brought as a present to the Empress Josephine from the Isle of France. It is described by Fred. Cuvier, and, like all the others, died a short time after it reached Europe. When first brought on board, it showed the same caution with Dr Abel's orang; would not mount aloft until it had seen M. Decaen, by whom it was brought up, do so—and during its life the same attachment to its owner, and annoyance in his absence, appeared. In eating or drinking, it would occasionally use its hands to convey the food or vessel to its lips, but would as often apply the lips to the food, and when drinking would lengthen them out—a power which it possessed in an extraordinary degree.

A spoon was sometimes given to it, with which in imitation it would attempt to lift the food; but when that could not be accomplished, the spoon would be significantly handed to the nearest person with whom it was acquainted. In the whole of its actions, the resemblance to Dr Abel's animal was so near, that a detail would be nearly a recapitulation. We refer. therefore, to the paper itself in the 15th volume of the Annales du Muséum d'Histoire Naturelle. One circumstance may be mentioned, of a singular attachment the animal took for two kittens. These it would carry under each arm to their great annoyance; it seemed to have pleasure also in placing them upon its head, but in this position the claws became troublesome from their restlessness, and were sometimes attempted to be pulled out. This could not be accomplished, but so much pleasure seemed to be experienced by the position, that the inconvenience of their scratches was afterwards unheeded.

The capture of an adult specimen of this animal, which we noticed at the commencement of our description, took place under the following circumstances, and places the fact of its immense size and strength beyond doubt; we are indebted also for it to the exertions of Dr Abel, who wrote an account of the remains of the animal for the Asiatic Researches.[*] It is so interesting that we insert it entire, and have added some illustrations of the skull and teeth from the plates accompanying that gentleman's narrative, and casts of them, which are in the Museum of the Royal Society of Edinburgh.

" A boat party under the command of Messrs Craygy-man and Fish, officers of the brig Mary-Anne-Sophia, having landed to procure water at a place called Ramboom, near Touraman, on the north-west coast of Sumatra, on a spot where there was much cultivated

* Asiatic Researches, vol. xv. p. 941.

ground and but few trees, discovered on one of them
a gigantic animal of the monkey tribe. On the approach of the party he came to the ground, and when
pursued sought refuge in another tree at some distance, exhibiting, as he moved, the appearance of a
tall man-like figure covered with shining brown hair,
walking erect with a waddling gait, but sometimes
accelerating his motion with his hands, and occasionally impelling himself forward with the bough of a
tree. His motion on the ground was plainly not his
natural mode of progression, for even when assisted
by his hands or a stick, it was slow and vacillating;
it was necessary to see him among trees, in order to
estimate his agility and strength. On being driven to
a small clump, he gained by one spring a very lofty
branch, and bounded from one branch to another with
the ease and alacrity of another monkey. Had the
country been covered with wood, it would have been
almost impossible to prevent his escape, as his mode
of travelling from one tree to another is described to
be as rapid as the progress of a swift horse. Even
amidst the few trees that were on the spot, his movements were so quick that it was very difficult to
obtain a settled aim, and it was only by cutting down
one tree after another, that his pursuers, by confining
him within a very limited range, were enabled to
destroy him by several successive shots, some of which
penetrated his body and wounded his viscera. Having
received five balls, his exertions relaxed, and, reclining

exhausted on one of the branches of a tree, he vomited
a considerable quantity of blood.   The ammunition
of the hunters being by this time expended, they
were obliged to fell the tree in order to obtain him,
and did this in full confidence that his power was so
far gone that they could secure him without trouble;
but were astonished, as the tree was falling, to see him
effect his retreat to another with apparently undi-
minished vigour.   In fact, they were obliged to cut
down all the trees before they could drive him to
combat his enemies on the ground, against whom he
still exhibited surprising strength and agility, although
he was at length overpowered by numbers, and destroyed by the thrusts of spears, and the blows of stones
and other missiles.   When nearly in a dying state,
he seized a spear made of a supple wood, which would
have withstood the strength of the stoutest man, and
shivered it in pieces; in the words of the narrator, he
broke it as if it had been a carrot.   It is stated by
those who aided in his death, that the human-like
expression of his countenance, and piteous manner of
placing his hands over his wounds, distressed their
feelings, and almost made them question the nature
of the act they were committing.   When dead, both
natives and Europeans contemplated his figure with
amazement.   His stature, at the least computation,
was upwards of six feet.

" By Captain Cornfoot, who furnished the details of
this animal to Dr Abel, he was said to be a full

head taller than any man on board, measuring seven
feet in what might be called his ordinary standing
posture, and eight feet when suspended for the purpose
of being skinned.

" It seems probable that the animal had travelled
from some distance to the place where he was found,
as his legs were covered with mud up to the knees,
and he was considered as great a prodigy by the
natives as by the Europeans.   They had never before
met with an animal like him, although they lived
within two days' journey of one of the vast and
almost impenetrable forests of Sumatra.   They seemed
to think that his appearance accounted for many
strange noises, resembling screams and shouts, and
various sounds, which they could neither attribute
to the roar of the tiger, nor to the voice of any other
beast with which they were familiar."

The following measurement was made by Dr Abel,
from the remains of the animal, which were deposited
in the Asiatic Society's Museum.   " The skin of the
body of the animal, dried and shrivelled up as it is,
measures, in a straight line from the top of the shoulder to the part where the ancle has been removed,
five feet ten inches ; the perpendicular length of the
neck, as it is in the preparation, three inches and a
half ; the length of the head, from the top of the forehead to the end of the chin, nine inches ; and the
length of the skin still attached to the foot, from the
line of its separation from the leg, eight inches : we

thus obtain seven feet six inches and a half as the
approximate height of the animal."

A description of the remains of this gigantic animal
is also given by Dr Abel.   " The face, with the
exception of the beard, is nearly bare, a few straggling
short downy hairs being alone scattered over it, and
is of a dark lead colour.   The eyes are small in relation to those of man, and are about an inch apart ;
the eyelids well fringed with lashes.   The ears are
one inch and a half in length, and barely an inch in
breadth, are closely applied to the head, and resemble
those of man, with the exception of wanting the lower
lobe.   The nose is scarcely raised above the level of
the face, and is chiefly distinguished by two nostrils,
three-fourths of an inch in breadth, placed obliquely
side by side.   The mouth projects considerably in a
mammillary form, and its opening is very large ; when
closed, the lips appear narrow, but are in reality half
an inch in thickness.   The hair of the head is of a
reddish-brown, grows from behind forwards, and is
five inches in length.   The beard is handsome, and
appears to have been curly in the animal's lifetime,
and approaches to a chestnut colour ; it is about three
inches long, springing very gracefully from the upper
lip near the angles of the mouth, in the form of mus-
taches ; when descending, it mixes with that of the
chin, the whole having a very wiry aspect ; the face
of the animal is much wrinkled."   The length of
the face, from the commencement of the hair on the

forehead to the setting on of the neck, was thirteen
inches and a half, and the other parts in a like remark.
able proportion.   The lower jaw with the teeth, is
given by Dr Abel of the natural size, and the figure
which we have copied on page 131 will give a better
idea of its magnitude than a detail of its mea-
-surement.   The annexed cut of the canine tooth
extracted, is taken from a cast in the Royal Society's

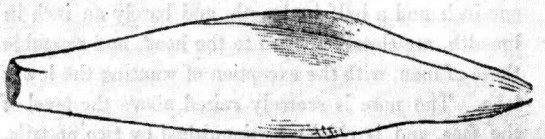

Museum in Edinburgh.   We add also a delineation
of the upper teeth, from a plate by Dr Abel, which

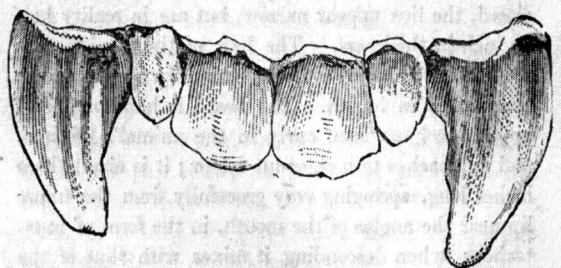

are remarkable for the breadth of the centre cutting
teeth, and the narrowness of the lateral ones; and in

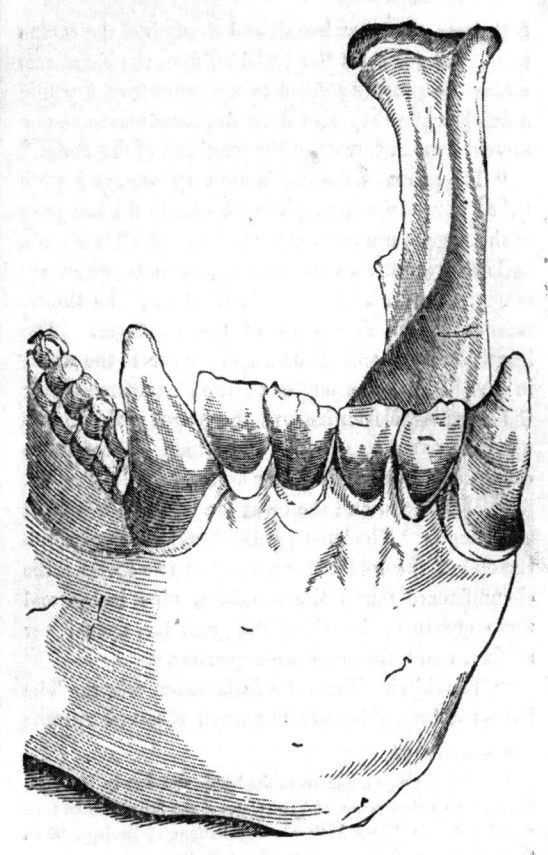

both jaws, the great length and strength of the canine teeth, will point out the variation from the characters which are generally given to the genus from a young animal, while they also show the resemblance to our sketch, from F. Cuvier, of the dentition of the Pongo.*

" The palms of the hands are very long, and quite naked from the wrists. Their backs, to the last joint of the fingers, are covered with hair, which inclines a little backwards ; all the fingers have nails, which are strong, convex, and of a black colour ; the thumb reaches to the first joint of the forefinger. The length from the end of the middle finger to the wrist, in a right line, was one foot ; the circumference over the knuckles, eleven inches ; the length of the thumb upon the palm, two inches and a half. The feet are covered with long brown hair on the back, to the last joint of the toes, and the great toe is set on nearly at right angles. The length of the foot, from the heel to the end of the middle toes, one foot two inches ; the circumference round the knuckles, nine inches and three quarters ; length of the great toe, upon lower surface, two inches and three quarters.†

" The skin itself was of a dark leaden colour. The hair of a brownish red ; but when observed at some

* See page 108.

† Reduced plates are given of the hands and feet by Dr Abel, in the Asiatic Researches, and two plates of the full size have been introduced into James Wilson's Illustrations of Zoology, taken from casts in the Museum of the Royal Society.

distance, has a dull, and, in some places, an almost black appearance.   It is on all parts very long ; on the fore-arm directed upwards, and on the upper arm downwards, but from its length, it hangs shaggy below ; from the shoulders it hangs in large and massy tufts, which, in continuation with the long hair on the back, seems to form one long mass to the very centre of the body. About the flanks the hair is equally long, and in the living animal must have descended below the thighs."

From the preceding details of the young red orang, and this gigantic Sumatran animal, the description of this singular creature may be considered as having attained a considerable degree of perfection.   It would be, however, of much importance, that a specimen having attained its maturity, could be procured and brought alive to this country, that an opportunity might be afforded of studying the disposition and temper.   The general impression at present is, that the docility and gentleness of the young becomes changed into ungovernable ferocity, and that the propensities of an animal become more and more developed by age.   How far this corresponds with the recession of the foreheads of the adult skulls, it would be interesting to trace ; and we can only hope that the perseverance of some enterprising traveller will erelong enable us to judge of these singular structures.

We have only now to notice the illustrations we have added to this already long article.   They were fortunately procured by the assistance of a clever draughts-

man, and are acknowledged to be correct represent-
ations.   The animal from which they were taken was
exhibited in Edinburgh by Mr Cops, in August last,
and our acknowledgements are due to that gentleman
for permitting the drawings to be made, and for his
polite attention in pointing out its peculiarities.

The general actions of this specimen also correspond-
ed with those above described ; his manner of progression was always assisted by the arms, resting his
knuckles on the floor of the apartment, and thus
having a resemblance to a person upon crutches.
After being brought into the room, he would seat, or
rather squat, himself on a sofa, and having judiciously
folded a blanket of flannel round him, would deliberately survey the visiters.   A checked shirt was
frequently thrown over him, which he wore with
great complacency.   One day a gentleman wearing
linen of a similar pattern appeared in the room, and
was immediately singled out, nor was the animal
satisfied until he was allowed to examine the shirt,
pulling it out from the breast, and holding it in comparison with that which covered himself, expressively
looking up in the gentleman's face, as if doubtful of
his right to a garb which agreed so nearly with his
own.

His motions were calm and sedate, with a semblance of timidity, and he did not exhibit that quickness and activity we are used to attribute to the
quadrumanous animals.   Two young boas were ex-

hibited in the room, which excited the greatest horror when taken from their covering, and a watch was incessantly kept up until they were again placed under restraint. This was also remarked of the specimen brought to the Empress Josephine. In their native wilds they are their most insidious enemy.

This animal was perfectly good-natured, and scarcely ever showed any inclination to anger. When not exhibited, he was allowed to go about the house, and was generally to be found playing with the children of the person with whom Mr Cops lodged, and they seemed mutually pleased with each other. In colour and proportions, he did not differ from those we have previously noticed.

The next form to which our attention is most naturally directed, as entering the group of *orangs*, is the Gibbons or long-armed apes, forming the genus *Hylobates** of Illiger. They may be generally characterised by having the same dentition, though some-

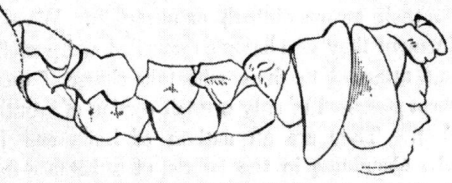

* Hylobates, *ὑλοβατης.* Walking through woods. — *Illig. Prod.* 109.

what modified in form, with the African and Asiatic
orangs, and represented in the annexed cut of the
dentition of the *H. leuciscus* ; in being destitute of a
tail ; and peculiarly remarkable from the great length
of the anterior extremities, which reach the ground
when the animal is placed in an erect position. Their
height scarcely exceeds four feet, and they never possess that gigantic and powerful form, which is attained in a native state by the animals we have just
described. Their dispositions in a wild state, appear
shy and timid. They are in most instances gregarious, and in this respect resemble the howling monkeys of America, which is farther confirmed by the
presence, in some, of the large guttural sacks, and the
continued howling which betrays their haunts. Some
species are possessed of very great activity, and use
their long arms with almost as much effect as the
long and prepensile tail of the Sapajous. Some appear
again to be more sluggish in their habits, but are
possessed of an acute sense of sight and hearing, and
will seldom allow an intruder to approach so near as to
render their escape difficult or uncertain. When in
confinement they soon become reconciled and peaceful,
become attached to those who take charge of them,
but seem possessed of only a small portion of intuitive
intellect. They are all natives of India and her
islands, abounding in the forests, at a distance from
which they are very seldom found ; and, when occasionally discovered straying, fall an easy prey, from

Stewart del.   *Lizars sc.*

HYLOBATES HOOLOCK.

(The Hoolock.)

their great timidity and awkwardness of progression
on a comparatively flat surface. The first we shall
mention, is a new species from the continent of
India.

THE HOOLOCK.

Hylobates hoolock.—HARLAN.

PLATE III.

Simia hoolock, *Harlan, Transactions of the American Philosophical Society*, Volume iv. N. S. Page 52.

THIS curious species was first noticed by a well-
known American naturalist, and is figured in the
work above quoted ; it wants the callosities on the
hips, and from its nearer approach in proportions to the
orangs, would take precedence in our system of the
other Gibbons.

It is a native of the Garrow Hills, in the vicinity of
Goalpara, in British India. The first description of
it is by Dr Harlan, taken from living specimens and
interesting letters which accompanied them, and detailed what had been observed regarding them in a
wild state. A specimen has lately been added to the
Museum of Edinburgh, which has served for our illus-

tration, to which we have added the letters of Dr
Burrough to its American describer.

It is strongly characterised as distinct from the
other long-armed orangs or Gibbons. In form, size,
and proportion, it is most closely allied to the female
of the active Gibbon, *H. agilis* of F. Cuvier; but is
very different in colours and markings, especially the
young individuals of the two species, which differ
totally in these respects. The male and female resemble each other in the present species; but the
sexes of the active Gibbon are different in size and
colour.

The specimen in the Edinburgh Collection agrees
nearly with that described by Dr Harlan.

The colour of the young, according to Dr Harlan,
is blackish brown, sprinkled with gray on the hands
and feet; the buttocks are grayish; a tuft of the same
colour extends along the middle of the front of the
body; the band of gray over the eyes of the adult, is
generally interrupted in the middle of the forehead by
a line of black hairs, which is absent in the young
one; the band is broader in the latter, in proportion of
seven-tenths to four-tenths. In this individual, about
half the size of the adult, a remarkable difference was
observed in the relative proportions of the arm and
fore-arm. In the young animal, the fore-arm is shorter
than the arm—a fact at variance with the proportions
of those parts, not only in the orangs, but in all the
race of adult *Simiœ*. In the adult, the arm and fore-

arm are within one inch two-tenths of being equal in length.

The dentition of this species nearly agrees with that of its congeners; but is remarkable in the length of the canine teeth.

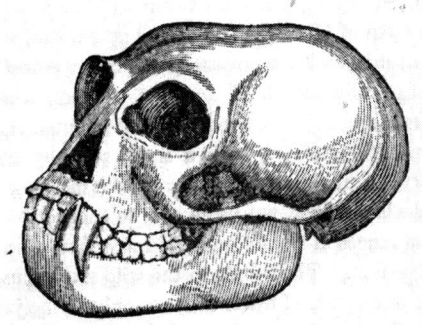

We now add the interesting letter of Dr Burrough accompanying the specimens described by Dr Harlan.

" The specimens of the orang-outang or Gibbons, furnished you, were obtained by me during my late excursion into the interior of Bengal.   They were presented to me by Captain Alexander Davidson, of the Honourable East India Company, stationed at Goalpara, situate on the Burrampooter river, in *Assam*. This district of country was formerly attached to the Burmese empire, but at present is in possession of the

East India Company, and constitutes the north-eastern limits of their territory in this quarter.

" The orang, of which I am now to speak, called by the Assamese ' Hoolock,' is to be met with on the Garrow Hills, in the vicinity of Goalpara, between latitudes 25° and 28° north; and the specimens brought to this country by me, were taken within a few miles of the town of Goalpara. The full grown one, which at this time you have prepared, was in my possession, alive, from the month of January to May, when it died from a blow it received across the lumbar region, inadvertently inflicted with a small stick by one of my servants at Calcutta. They inhabit more particularly the lower hills, not being able to endure the cold of those ranges of the Garrows of more than 4 or 500 feet elevation. Their food, in the wild state, consists, for the most part, of fruits common only to the jungle in this district of country; and they are particularly fond of the seeds and fruits of that sacred tree of India, called the Peopul-tree, and which, on the Garrow Hills, attains a very large size. They likewise take of some species of grass, and also the tender twigs and leaves of the Peopul and other trees, which they chew, swallow the juice thereof, and reject the indigestible part. They are easily tamed; and when first taken show no disposition to bite unless provoked to anger, and even then manifest a reluctance to defend themselves, preferring to retreat into some corner rather than attack their enemy. They walk erect; and,

when placed upon a floor or in an open field, balance
themselves very prettily, by raising their hands over
their head, and slightly bending their arm at the wrist
and elbow, and then run tolerably fast, rocking from
side to side; and if urged to greater speed, they let
fall their hands to the ground, and assist themselves
forward, rather jumping than running, still keeping
the body, however, nearly erect; if they succeed in
making their way to a grove of trees, they then swing
with such astonishing rapidity from branch to branch,
and from tree to tree, that they are soon lost in the
jungle or forest.

" The individual in question became so tame and
manageable in less than a month, that he would take
hold of my hand and walk with me, helping himself
along at the same time with the other hand applied to
the ground, as described above. He would come at
my call, and seat himself in a chair by my side at the
breakfast-table, and help himself to an egg, or the
wing of a chicken from my plate, without endangering
any of my table furniture. He would partake of
coffee, chocolate, milk, tea, &c.; and although his
usual mode of taking liquids was by dipping his
knuckles into the cup and licking his fingers, still,
when apparently more thirsty, he would take up the
vessel from which I fed him with both hands, and
drink like a man from a spring. His principal food
consisted of boiled rice, boiled bread and milk, with
sugar, plantains, bananas, oranges, &c., all of which

he ate, but seemed best pleased with bananas. **He
was** fond of insects; would search in the crevices of
my house for spiders, and if a fly chanced to come in
his reach, he would dexterously catch him in one hand,
generally using his right hand. Like many of the
different religious castes of this country, he seemed to
entertain an antipathy to an indiscriminate use of
animal food, and would not eat of either the flesh of
the cow or hog; would sometimes taste a little piece
of beef, but never eat of it. I have seen him take
fried fish, which he seemed to relish better than almost
any other description of animal food, with the exception of chicken, and even this he would eat but very
sparingly of, preferring his common diet, bread and
milk, with sugar, fruit, &c. In temper he was remarkably pacific, and seemed, as I thought, often glad
to have an opportunity of testifying his affection and
attachment for me. When I visited him in the
morning, he would commence a loud and shrill whoo
—whoo—whoo—whoo, which he would keep up often
from five to ten minutes, with an occasional intermission for the purpose of taking a full respiration; until
finally, apparently quite exhausted, he would lie
down and allow me to comb his head, and brush the
long hair on his arms, and seem delighted with the
tickling sensation produced by the brush on his belly
and legs. He would turn from side to side, first hold
out one arm and then the other, and when I attempted
to go away, he would catch hold of my arm or coat-

tail, and pull me back again to renew my little attentions to him, daily bestowed. If I called to him from
a distance, and he could recognise my voice, he would
at once set up his usual cry which he sometimes
gradually brought down to a kind of moan, but generally resumed his louder tone when I approached him.
This animal was a male, but showed no particular
marks of the sex; and by a casual glance, might
readily, if not examined more closely, have passed for
a female. I have no idea of his age; but, judging from
the size and length of his canine teeth, suppose him
to have been advanced in life.

"The other large ' Hoolock,' of which you have
the cranium, was also a male, and full grown. He
was likewise obtained from the Garrow Hills, in
Assam, presented to me by my friend Captain A.
Davidson of Goalpara. He came into my possession
in the month of April, and died at sea in July, just
before getting up with the Cape of Good Hope, of a
catarrhal affection. His death probably might have
been hastened from want of proper food; such as is not
procurable on long voyages. This animal was similar
in habit and general characters to the one already
described; and may have been eight or ten years of
age, or perhaps older; as I am informed by the natives
of Assam they live to the age of twenty-five or thirty
years.

" The young specimen was also alive in my possession. This is a female, and was brought to me by a

Garrow Indian at the same time the first was received; but died on the way from Goalpara to Calcutta, of a pulmonary disease following catarrh. This poor little creature, when first taken sick, suffered great pain and oppression at the chest, for which I prescribed a cathartic of castor oil and calomel, and a warm bath, which seemed to afford it some temporary relief, but she died after ten days' illness. The animal appeared delighted with the bath; and when I removed her from the vessel, she would run back again to the water, and lie down again until again removed. She was like the others I had in my possession, gentle and pacific in disposition, very timid and shy of strangers; but in less than a week from the time she was taken, would, if put down in an open place, quickly run to me, jump in my arms, and hug me round the neck. I supposed her to have been from nine months to a year old. I fed her on boiled milk, goat's milk diluted with water and sweetened with sugar-candy. She also would sometimes partake of a little bread and milk, with the older one. She soon learned to suck the milk from a small bottle, through a quill covered with a piece of rag."

We shall next describe a very singular species from the East Indian Islands.

Stewart delt.   Lizars sc.

HYLOBATES SYNDACTYLA.

[The Siamang.]

THE SIAMANG.

Hylobates syndactyla.—RAFFLES.

PLATE IV.

Simia syndactyla, the Siamang, *Sir Stamford Raffles, Transactions of Linnæan Society*, vol. xiii. page 241; *Horsfield, Zoological Researches in Java.*—Le Siamang, *Frederic Cuvier, Histoire Naturelle des Mammiferes.*—Le Siamang, *Cuvier, Regne Animal*, vol. i. page 90.

THE Siamang, by some naturalists, has been separated from the other long-armed apes on account of the curious formation of the feet. They have the first and second toes closely united, as far as the middle of the second phalanx.

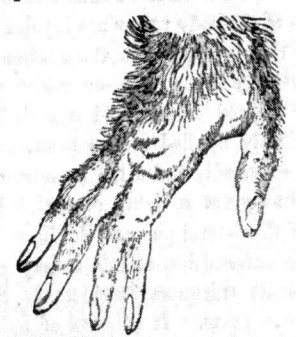

It was discovered by Sir Stamford Raffles in Sumatra,
and is particularly abundant in the vicinity of Bencoolen.
It is about three feet in height, and is entirely of a jet
black colour, with a few scattered grayish hairs on the
cheeks and chin.   The hair upon the body is shining,
long, soft, and thick.   The face is black, the muzzle
short, and the facial angle from 60° to 65°.   The nose
is flat and depressed above, but rises below abruptly,
with a cartilaginous eminence, in which the large,
nearly circular nostrils, are pierced from the sides in
an oblique direction ; at its extremity this eminence
is obtuse, and united to the upper lip by a narrow
gradually attenuated apex, which, forming a cartilaginous arch, gives a peculiar character to the Siamang.
The orbital margin is very prominent ; and the frontal
bone rises above the eyes obliquely, with a very gradual inclination backward.   This part is covered with
hairs, which have a different character from those on
other parts of the body ; they are regular and straight,
and, being closely applied to the surface of the head,
form a gradually rising plain, on which the hair appears as if dressed or rendered smooth by art.   The
ears are closely applied to the head, are margined,
and have externally the same structure as in man.
They are in a great measure concealed by the hairy
covering of the lateral parts of the head, which, with
that of the extremities, affords a very peculiar character, and its thickness considerably increases the
bulk of these parts.   It consists of hairs close and

woolly near the skin, united in small tufts, which diverge irregularly, and form a shaggy fleece. The separate hairs are above two inches long, and on every part except the head are slightly curved, so as to cause a somewhat frizzled appearance. The mouth is large, extending almost from cheek to cheek. The throat appears very broad, and has the outward appearance of a swoln goitre destitute of hair; this is the large guttural sack, which has been thought to assist the production of the wild continued howling of some monkeys, and which appears inflated when the animal cries. In the females the breast is destitute of hair; but the species appears to be subject to little of the variation incident to so many of this tribe from age or sex. The fingers of the hands are very slender, and of uncommon length; and the formation of the feet, as we have previously mentioned, is the most remarkable variation from the other Gibbons.*

The active time of the Siamang is at daybreak and twilight, when they are found assembled in large bands, and make the forests resound with their howl, in a manner concerted, which is often heard at an immense distance. During the day they remain quiet and inactive, and utter no cries unless disturbed. By the Malays they are supposed to be conducted by a head or chief, which is always the strongest, and which is also supposed to be invulnerable. He is

* We are indebted to Dr Horsfield's Researches in Java for much of this information.

K

thought to direct their motions and to preside at
their morning and evening howlings.   In their general
habits they are said to be more sluggish and inactive
than some which we shall presently describe; and
they neither swing from the branches, or leap with
that surprising agility, which characterise some of
the others. They seem, however, sensible of their
imperfections ; and being endowed with an acute
sense of hearing, fly to their retreats upon the least
noise which is not familiar to them.   If any members
of.a band are wounded, they are immediately left behind ; a mother only will remain with the young one
if hurt, and will allow herself to be taken rather than
fly alone.   MM. Diard and Duvancel relate, that this
maternal affection is at all times remarkably strong,
and not exercised only in a time of danger. The
young are tended with the greatest care ; and these
gentlemen mention having seen the females carry their
young to the banks of a stream, wash them notwithstanding their cries, and wipe and dry them in the
most careful manner.

These gentlemen also describe their habits when
confined, as characterised by stupidity, dulness, and
inactivity, in a few days becoming mild, and deprived
of all ferocity, but always timid, and without that
familiarity and impudence which so many of this
tribe very soon acquire ; nor does either good or bad
treatment seem to have much effect on their dispositions.   The most common position is sitting squatted,

surrounded by their long arms, and having the head concealed between their limbs. Dr Horsfield mentions, on the contrary, that a Siamang in the possession of Sir Stamford Raffles, was remarkably tame and tractable, and was never happy but when allowed to be in company with some one; and another described by Mr George Bennet, from observations made during a voyage from India to this country, showed a lively affection towards himself and those who behaved kindly to it.* Sir Stamford Raffles mentions having seen a specimen entirely white.

The other animals contained in this group have naked callosities on the buttocks, like the baboons, and in their dispositions are more active. One of the first known, though till lately involved in obscurity, is the *Simia lar* of Linnæus; the long-armed ape of Pennant. This was thought to be subject to a variation in the colour of the wrists and hands to white; but the distinction has turned out to be that of different species, and for that with white hands M. Geoffroy Saint Hilaire has retained the old name of *lar*, while the totally black species has been dedicated by the same gentleman to Sir Stamford Raffles, under the name of *Hylobates Rafflesii*. Another animal allied to these, and generally described as a variety under the title of *Lesser Gibbon*, seems yet to be held

* See that gentleman's interesting description in Loudon's Magazine of Natural History, vol. v. p. 131.

as a subject for doubt by our most modern zoologists;
it is much less in size, and has generally been procured from Malacca.   There is a sixth species, somewhat allied except in colour, which, by older writers,
was also confounded with the long-armed gibbon; it is
the *Moloch* or *Wow-wow*, the *Hylobates leuciscus* of
moderns.   It inhabits the Moluccas, is entirely of a
grayish white, except the face, which is black, but
does not differ in general habit from its congeners.

The only remaining animal we have to mention, as
embraced in this group, is also known under the name
of *Wow-wow*, but which is indiscriminately applied
by the natives of the Indian islands to several species
though they are distinguished from one another by
additional names.   It is remarkably contrasted from
the others by its more pleasing shades of colouring
and surprising agility.   We give a plate of the female
and young of

PLATE 5.

Stewart delt   Lizars sc.

HYLOBATES AGILIS. Female.

(The Active Gibbon)

THE ACTIVE GIBBON.

Hylobates agilis.—F. Cuvier.

Plate V.

Le Wow-wow, *Frederic Cuvier, Histoire Naturelle des Mammiferes.*—Hylobates agilis, the Active Gibbon, *Griffith, Animal Kingdom,* vol. v.—Le Gibbon Brun, *Cuvier, Regne Animal,* vol. i. p. 90.

This very active animal inhabits the forests of Sumatra, where it is known under the name of *Ungaputi.* It appears to have been first noticed by Sir Stamford Raffles, to whom specimens were brought by MM. Diard and Duvancel, who were for many years in the pay and employment of this most assiducus naturalist. These gentlemen also sent specimens to the Paris Collections, which served as copies for Frederic Cuvier, in his great and elegant work upon the Mammaliæ, and which we have freely used in the progress of our present little volume. M. Duvancel also sent to Paris descriptions, which were used for the above-mentioned work, and which are now united with what information we have been able to procure elsewhere.

The face is naked, and of a bluish-black. In the
male, the cheeks and a superciliary band are of a
yellowish-white, beautifully contrasting with the clear
chocolate-brown of the upper half of the body; these
marks are wanting in the female represented on
our plate. The lower extremities are of the same dark
colour, and the lower part of the back, and fore part
of the thighs, are of a yellowish-brown. The shade of
the colour, of both the dark and light parts, however,
vary considerably according to age, and the light parts
above, sometimes occupy a greater or lesser space. The
hair in healthy animals is clear and fine, except upon
the neck, where it becomes lengthened, and somewhat woolly or curled. The young are always
much paler in colour than the adults, or those at an
advanced age, and the very young animals are of a
uniform yellowish-white. The general height scarcely
exceeds two feet seven or eight inches, and the arms
reach the ground when the animal stands erect.

They are endowed with surprising agility, and
their light form and slender-looking extremities
hardly give an idea of the great muscularity which
they must possess. If the extreme tree on the borders
of a forest can be reached by them, it will be in vain
to pursue farther; they swing, leap, and, as it were,
throw themselves from one tree to another, clearing
at times a space of forty feet, with a rapidity
which defies any pedestrian pursuer. When a
slender branch can be grasped, the body is swung

several times, until sufficient impetus is gained, and they then dart off with the utmost apparent ease and grace.

In a state of domestication, they are not so lively as many other monkeys, though susceptible of some cultivation; they are easily frightened, and as easily again reassured, fond of being caressed, inquisitive and familiar, and sometimes playful. In the internal anatomy, they differ from the preceding species in the absence of the guttural sack; nevertheless, the cry is nearly similar, which must show that this formation is not necessary to produce the *howl* of this and some other monkeys, or that some other structure must fill up the deficiency.

We have now mentioned all the known species of long-armed apes or Gibbons, and there are two forms which by most zoologists have been placed immediately following them, of which we have been unable to see specimens. We shall therefore shortly notice them from the works of highest reputation, before proceeding to the Guenons or long-tailed monkeys of the Old World. The first has been characterised by Eschscholtz, under the name of *Prebytis;* * possesses no cheek-pouches; has naked callosities; the arms reach to the knees, and the tail is of considerable length. The facial angle 60°. Only one species has been discovered in Sumatra, *P. mitrula,* or capped mon-

* Πρισβις, an old woman. So called from the resemblance of an old woman with a cap.

key ; of small size, above of a bluish-green, beneath grayish-white.

The second is named *Colobus* by Illiger,* remarkable for having only four fingers upon the upper extremities, and in this respect representing *Ateles*† of the New World, to which it also comes near in the shortness of the muzzle, and comparative shortness of the face. In other respects it resembles the Guenons.

Three species are described. They are natives of Africa, but little is known of their habits or locality.

The type of this genus may be seen in the *Simia polycomos*, Schreber, the full-bottomed monkey of Pennant, black, with longer hair covering the neck, in the form of a mane. It inhabits the forests of Guinea and Sierra Leone. The next is the bay monkey, *Colobus ferruginosus*, which has been thought by some to be merely a variety of the preceding ; and the third is an unfigured species, dedicated by M. Kuhl to M. Temminck (*Colobus Temminckii*, Kuhl.) It formed part of the collection of Mr Bullock, and, at the dispersion of that valuable museum, passed to that of Temminck. The upper parts of the head, neck, back, and shoulders, black, the limbs clear reddish, and the under parts having a tinge of tawny yellow. The native country unknown.

It may be remarked that this genus is placed by Illiger after the *Cynocephali*, and next that of *Ateles*,

---

* Κολοβος, maimed, imperfect
† Ατελης, imperfect.

with which the monkeys of the New World are commenced.

THE GUENONS.

Following for our guidance the arrangement of the quadrumanous animals proposed by Cuvier, whose extensive experience and varied research, entitle him to every confidence, we shall proceed next with his brother's sub-family of the Guenons, or long-tailed monkeys of the Old World. Most zoologists place them after the orangs and gibbons, and reach the baboons by those species where the muzzle becomes more lengthened, (*Cercocebus sabeus*, &c.,) by the Rhesus monkey* and Barbary ape, and thus reach the *Cynocephali*, which have the largest facial angle, the nostrils placed at the extremity of the muzzle, possess a less degree of intelligence, and have dispositions akin to the fiercest and most brutal. With these they conclude the forms of the Old World.

The large assortment of animals which have been placed in this group, may be termed the most agreeable of the " monkey race." They embrace considerable variety of shape and size, but often exhibit furs of the greatest brightness and beauty, with forms at once light and graceful ; while their dispositions are in general mild, peaceful, and affectionate, or, if occa-

* See vignette titlepage.

generally riotous, are confined to displays of playfulness and mischief, and are entirely free from the fierce and malignant tempers displayed in a greater or less degree among all the baboons. When taken at an early age they are readily tamed, and become playful and familiar; they are extremely agile, though generally calm and circumspect in their motions, and learn a variety of tricks, which they perform with much cunning and address. In a wild state they are gregarious, and, bird-like, inhabit the rich forests of Africa and Asia.

The divisions which Frederic Cuvier has proposed, are entitled by him *Semnopitheques* and *Guenons*. The former he places next to the Gibbons, which some of the species so much resemble in different parts of the skeleton, as to be with difficulty recognised, and designates them *Semnopithecus*, from the grave and serious character of the animals contained in it. But before proceeding with these, we shall describe two monkeys, which, though generally admitted into the *Guenon* group, are so imperfectly known as to render any classification, however near we may come in our analogical reasonings, to be uncertain. The first of these is

PLATE 6.

Stewart delt.   Lizars sc.

NASALIS LARVATUS.

(The Kahau or Proboscis Monkey.)

THE KAHAU OR PROBOSCIS MONKEY.

Nasalis larvatus.—GEOFFROY.

PLATE VI.

Proboscis Monkey, *Pennant's Quadrupeds*, append. p. 322. —
Le Kahau, *Audibert, Histoire Naturelle des Singes.*—Nasalis
larvatus, *Geoffroy Saint Hilaire, Annales du Museum,* vol.
xix. p. 91.—Guenon nasique, *Desmaret's Mammalogie,* p. 55.

THIS singular monkey is at once distinguished
by the extraordinary elongation of the nose, which
is nearly four inches in length, and gives a grotesque
appearance to the animal, at the same time far
from pleasing. In other respects it presents a form of
considerable interest to the zoologist ; the body is un-
shapely, protruding in front like the Orangs, and wants
the lightness possessed by so many of the Guenons.
The arms are of very considerable proportional length,
like the Gibbons ; and, like the howling monkeys, it
possesses a large guttural sack—while the presence
of a lengthened tail, and of naked callosities, present
altogether a very curious combination.

The kahau is about three feet in height when
placed in an erect position, and, with the exception

of the tail and lower part of the back, is of a reddish-
brown colour.   The female is said, by Audibert, to
want the light-coloured markings on the back, and to
be rather less in size; the nose and face are of a
blackish-brown colour, the nostrils are placed at
the extremity, and they can be blown up or swelled

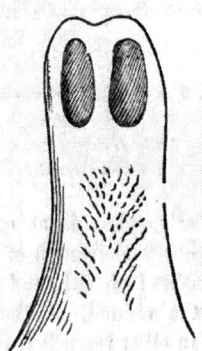

Nose seen from beneath, from Audibert.

to a considerable size.   Messrs Vigors and Horsfield
have given the profile of another monkey, brought
from the Island of Borneo, in which the nose is
scarcely one-third of the length, and is somewhat
turned up.*   They suspect that this is the young of
the proboscis monkey, which, if correct, will show
that the elongation is much dependent upon the age

* Zoological Journal, No. XIII. p. 110.

of the individuals ; while, should farther examination
prove that it is really distinct, they propose to designate
it as a second species, under the title of *N. recurvus,*
or turned-up proboscis monkey.

The kahau is a native of the Island of Borneo, and
is still rare in collections.   It is a gregarious animal,
and is said to assemble in large troops, at sunrise and
sunset, upon the trees bordering rivers.   They are
possessed of great activity, and dart from tree to tree,
springing to a distance of fifteen or twenty feet.   They
utter continued cries, somewhat similar to the expression of the common name which has been applied to
them.

Our plate is taken from that of Audibert.

The other animal we alluded to, which appears to
possess all the characteristics of the first division of
the *Guenons,* is,

THE DOUC OR COCHIN-CHINA MONKEY.

Lasiopyga * *nemea.*—ILLIGER.

PLATE VII.

Simia nemæus, *Linnæus.*—Pygathrix nemæus, *Geoffroy Saint Hilaire, Annales du Museum,* vol. xix. p. 90.—Le Douc, *Audibert, Histoire Naturelle des Singes.*—Guenon Douc, *Desmarets' Mammalogie,* p. 54.

THIS singularly but beautifully marked species has been the subject of discussion among many naturalists, and its great rarity prevents, even to the present period, a satisfactory examination of its form and structure ; by some it is placed at the commencement of this division, while by others it is stationed at the conclusion, to be followed by the lesser baboons. Illiger gives the characters of his genus, so as, in fact, to include some of the latter, but by Geoffroy it is placed as the solitary representative of his genus above mentioned. It is a native of Cochin-China, and as very few specimens have yet reached Europe, little or nothing is known regarding it. The height is about two feet,

---

* Lasiopyga—λασιος, hairy ; πυγη, buttocks, posteriors.

Stewart del.ᵗ   Lizars sc.

LASIOPYGA NEMEA.

[The Douc or Cochin China Monkey.]

and a reference to the annexed plate will best explain the varied colours of the fur. It is engraved from that of Audibert, taken from a specimen in the Paris Museum. Its principal characteristics are the great proportional length of the upper extremities, and the absence of callosities on the hips.

Having mentioned these two singular animals, we shall proceed with the first division of the Guenon group, the *Semnopitheci.* The most striking external characters are the flatness of the face; small cheek pouches; the length of the body, and slenderness of the extremities; the great length of the tail, and the little bare space upon the hips; while the system of dentition presents a marked difference from the next form included in the group. Annexed is a view of the dentition of *S. maurus,* from Frederic Cuvier's

work, but which exhibits the canine teeth of less size

than the specimen figured by Dr Horsfield.   The canine tooth is there exhibited, standing nearly one-

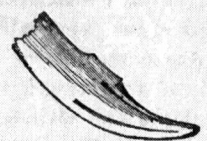

half longer than the others, and grooved on the inner surface.   The chief difference in the molar teeth is in the posterior grinder of the lower jaw having distinctly

five points, which distinguishes it from *Cercopithecus*, and which will be better understood by comparing the cuts now introduced with those accompanying the true Guenons.

Dr Horsfield had taken the Negro monkey as the type of this form, whereas F. Cuvier selects another animal as more characteristic; and we are the more inclined to follow this arrangement, as the Doctor himself observes that *S. maurus* is more robust in make than its congeners, and the slender proportions are one of the first characters which strike the attention.   The animal we allude to is,

PLATE 8.

SEMNOPITHECUS MELALOPHAS.

(The Simpia.)

Stewart delt.

Lizars sc.

THE SIMPAI.

Semnopithecus melalophos.—F. CUVIER.

PLATE VIII.

Simpai of Javanese ;—Simia melalophos, *Sir Stamford Raffles,*
Transactions Linnæan Society, vol. xiii. ;—*Frederic Cuvier,*
Histoire Naturelle des Mammiferes.

THIS monkey, a native of Java and Sumatra, was
first noticed by Sir Stamford Raffles, and afterwards
figured and described by F. Cuvier, from specimens
procured from the same sources.

According to the latter naturalist, the flatness of
the face is very remarkable; and if the facial angle
and size of the brow can be depended on as characteristics of intelligence, that of this animal ought to
be capable of greater developement than the orang-
outang. There are, however, few records of its habits
or dispositions; and we refer to the accompanying
plate for an idea of the form and colours. The length
of the adult animal to the insertion of the tail, is about
one foot six inches; the tail alone is between two and
three feet.

Another monkey very characteristic of this group is,

THE ENTELLUS MONKEY.

Semnopithecus entellus.—F. Cuvier.

PLATE IX.

Semnopithecus entellus, *Frederic Cuvier, Histoire Naturelle des Mammiferes ;—Gardens and Menagerie of Zoological Society,* vol. i. p. 80.—L'Entelle, *Audibert, Histoire Naturelle des Singes.*

The Entellus monkey, still of very rare occurrence in the European collections, presents a very remarkable form in its slender proportions, and the light colour of its fur, contrasted with the black skin of the face and extremities. It is a native generally of the Indian archipelago and some parts of the continent ; and, upon comparison of the relations of travellers, must abound in many parts of these countries, where they are venerated, or at least looked upon with a kind of superstitious awe, which prevents the natives from destroying them, and makes them often suffer from their depredations. They seem particularly susceptible of cold, which may account for their being seldom seen in our British menageries. Specimens which have been sent to Paris, and that in the Zoological

Stewart del.

Invart sc

SEMNOPITECUS ENTELLUS.

(The Entellus Monkey.)

Gardens, only survived a short period after their arrival in Europe; and one mentioned by Thunberg soon died of cold in the comparatively warm climate of the Cape of Good Hope.

The height of the Entellus described by F. Cuvier, is about one foot five inches; the length of the tail about two feet. The description of the specimen which died in the Zoological Gardens, by Mr Bennet, is as follows; and it may be remarked, that the only variation which seems incident to them is a yellow or redder tinge of the whitish fur.

" When taken at an early age they are readily tamed, become playful and familiar, are extremely agile, although generally calm and circumspect in their motions, and learn to perform a variety of tricks, which they execute with no little cunning and address. After a time, however, their playfulness wears off; their confidence is succeeded by mistrust; their agility settles down into a listless apathy; and, instead of resorting as before to the resources of their ingenuity for carrying any particular point, they have recourse to the brute force which they have acquired in its stead. At length they become as mischievous, and sometimes even as dangerous, as any of those monkeys which in their young state offer no such indications of good temper and intelligence.

" It is of a uniform ashy-gray on the upper parts, becoming darker on the tail, which is grayish-brown, of equal thickness throughout, and terminated by a few long hairs ru.ming out into a kind of point, but not forming a tuft.　The under surface of the body is of a dingy yellowish-white ; and the fore-arms, hands, and feet, are of a dusky black.　The fingers of both extre-mities are very long, and the thumbs comparatively short.　The face, which is black, with somewhat of a violet tinge, is surmounted, above the eyebrows, by a line of long stiff black hairs, which project forwards, and slightly upwards.　On the sides of the cheeks and beneath the chin, it is margined by a beard of grayish-white passing along the line of the jaws, and extending upwards in front of the ears, which are large and prominent, and of the same colour as the face.　The hairs of the fore part of the breast appear to diverge from a common centre.　The height of our specimen, which was not yet adult, when in a sitting posture exceeded two feet ; and his tail, which he rarely dis-played at its full length, but more usually kept curled up in a single coil, measured nearly three."

The foregoing details will point out the characters of this group.　Three other species are introduced into Desmarets' work, and in Griffith's Synopsis, under the names of *S. comatus,* somewhat allied to that now described, *S. pruinores,* approaching to the *Semno-pithecus maurus* of Dr Horsfield, which we shall now notice.

The Negro monkey, like its congeners, is a native of Java and Sumatra.　The length of the body is about two feet three inches, that of the tail nearly the same, and the form and proportions are more robust than in those we have mentioned for our type. From the want of a figure of this curious animal, Dr Horsfield's minute description may not be unacceptable.

"The covering of the Negro monkey, in adult subjects, is intensely black on every part, except the breast, the abdomen, the inner side of the extremities, and the root of the tail; these parts are gray. On the crown of the head, the black hairs are slightly tipped with gray; and as age advances, the gray portion becomes more extensive, and also shows itself on the upper parts of the body, but the extremities exteriorly, and the tail, even in the oldest subjects, retain their blackness. The hairs are remarkably long, delicate, soft, and silky. On the sides of the head, they are disposed backwards with a slight inclination outward, and they completely conceal the ears. They rise with a gradual slope on the forehead, but on the crown of the head they are suddenly deflected, so as to form a dependent crest. On the back, and on the extremities, they lie smooth and close. They are greatly elongated on the sides of the body, between the shoulders, so as to hang down to a considerable length when the animal walks on all fours. On the breast anteriorly, and on the abdomen, they are short, lax, and straggling.

"In its young state it exhibits a great contrast to that in the adult. Immediately after birth, our animal has a fulvous or reddish-yellow colour; as it advances in age, the colour gradually changes. A gray discoloration first shows itself on the hands, the forehead, and the tip of the tail; from these parts it gradually extends to the neck, the shoulders, and the flanks, and assumes from time to time a darker hue, until the coat of the animal is jet black above, and gray underneath.

" The face is regularly circumscribed by hairs, which are long, and closely applied to the head; the forehead, which is gradually sloping, is entirely concealed by them. The orbits of the eye are rather prominent; and the bones of the nose short. The nose consists of an angular ridge, which is considerably elevated between the eyes, and terminates without any fleshy protuberance, by a membrane which is gradually attenuated below, and on each side of which the nostrils are placed. These are large, oblong, slightly curved, and pass backward into the cranium in a horizontal direction. From the termination of the nose to the mouth a considerable space intervenes; but the lips are small and thin, so as to exhibit, when slightly retracted, the interior of the mouth. The chin is short and small; a circle of gray hairs encloses the mouth in the adult animal; and on the chin the hairs have a disposition downward, so as to exhibit the appearance of a beard. The upper part of the face is nearly naked; a few straggling stiff hairs are scattered on the cheeks and the upper lip, and on the more prominent part of the nose an interrupted series is observed. The irides of the eyes are of a dark brown colour. The ears are concealed from view by the long hairs which cover the lateral parts of the head; they are margined, and both in form and disposition of external parts closely resemble these organs in man. The neck is short, and considerably contracted. The trunk is of great length, broad and robust about the shoulders and the breast, and gradually of smaller dimensions towards the loins. The buttocks are marked with very large rough callosities. The mammæ, in the adult female, are lengthened and cylindrical. The tail is as long as the body and head taken together; in some individuals, and particularly in young subjects, it exceeds these parts in length; it is cylindrical during the greater part of its length; the base is gradually tapering, and the tip is thickened, and terminated by a close tuft of long hairs of an ovate form.

" The *Semnopithecus maurus* is distinguished among the Javanese by the name of Budeng, from another species which has the same form and habit, but a different external covering. The name of the latter is Lutung; but the Malays and Europeans apply this name to both species, and distinguish them by the epithet of black and red; the Budeng being denominated *Lutung itam,* and the Lutung of the Javanese, *Lutung mera.* In Sumatra the name of the ' Maure' is Lotong.

" The Budeng, or the black species, is much more abundant than the Lutung, or the red species; and the latter, both on account of its variety and comparative beauty, is a favourite among the natives. Whenever an individual is obtained, care is taken to domesticate it, and it is treated with kindness and attention. The Budeng, on the contrary, is neglected and despised; it requires much patience in any degree to improve the natural sullenness of its temper. In confinement it remains during many months grave and morose; and as it contributes nothing to the amusement of the natives, it is rarely found in villages, or about the dwellings. This does not arise from any aversion on the part of the Javanese to the monkey race; the most common species of the island, the *Cercocebus aygula* of Geoffroy, the *Egret* of Pennant, is very generally domesticated; and a favourite custom of the natives is to associate it with the horse. In every stable, from that of a prince to that of a mantry, or chief of a village, one of these monkeys is found; but I never observed the Budeng thus distinguished.

" The *Semnopithecus maurus* is found in abundance in the extensive forests of Java; it forms its dwelling on trees, and associates in numerous societies. Troops, consisting of more than fifty individuals, are often found together. In meeting them in the forests, it is prudent to observe them at a distance. They emit loud screams on the approach of man; and by the violent bustle and commotion excites by their movements, branches of decaying trees are not unfrequently detached, and precipitated on the spectators. They are often chased by the natives for the purpose of obtaining their fur. In these pursuits, which are generally ordered and attended by the chiefs, the animals are attacked with cudgels and stones, and cruelly destroyed in great numbers. The skins are prepared by a simple process, which the natives have acquired from the Europeans, and they conduct it at present with great skill. It affords a fur of a jet black colour, covered with long silky hairs, which is usefully employed both by the natives and the Europeans in preparing riding equipages and military decorations.

" The Budeng, during its young state, feeds on tender leaves of plants and trees; and when adult on wild fruits of every description, which are found in great abundance in the forests which it inhabits."

The last animal to be introduced here is one also figured in Dr Horsfield's Java, under the name of *Semnopithecus pyrrhus*. It is closely allied to the preceding in form and size, but differs in being of a clear reddish-brown, and is given by this distinguished zoologist with some doubt as distinct; but the different name by which it is known among the natives, and the permanency of its shades, he thinks, will entitle it to separation.

We now come to Frederic Cuvier's second great

division of the true *Guenons,* comprising the genera
Cercopithecus and *Cercocebus* of Geoffroy.   The manners are very nearly similar; but the graduation of
the facial angle, the large cheek-pouches, and shorter
tail of the latter, seem to lead gradually to the baboons.
The system of dentition also allies them by the length
of the canine teeth; and the annexed cut may be compared with those illustrating the preceding genus *Sem-*
nopithecus.

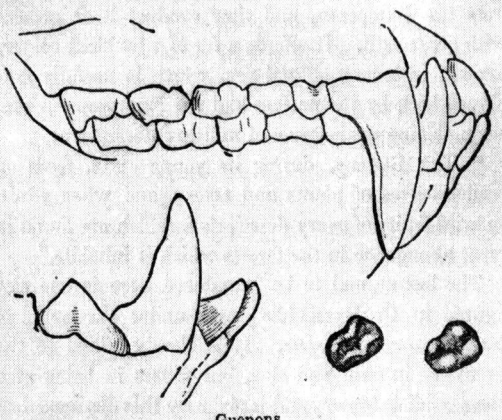

Guenons.

We shall first notice *Cercopithecus.*—In form it is
very closely allied to the last; but differs from both it
and the following by the large facial angle of from 50°
to 55°, rounded heads, flat noses, and long posterior
extremities.   The manners are also similar; but the

PLATE 10.

Stewart delt.

Lizars sc.

CERCOPITHECUS MONA.

(The Varied Monkey.)

animals comprised under it are more remarkable for grace of form, and beauty of colouring, and its type has been eulogized as elegant in the highest degree, mild of disposition, affectionate, and penetrating; and possessing every quality that could adorn the disposition of an animal. The species we allude to is,

THE VARIED MONKEY.

Cercopithecus mona.—GEOFFROY.

PLATE X.

The Varied Monkey, *Pennant's Quadrupeds*, page 210.—La Mone, *Audibert, Histoire Naturelle des Singes.*—*Frederic Cuvier, Histoire Naturelle des Mammiferes.*—Guenon Mone, *Desmarets' Mammologie*, p. 58.

THE Mona, says Frederic Cuvier, is superior to all the Guenons in the elegance of its form, and grace of its movements, the mildness of its disposition, the delicacy of understanding, and sagacity of countenance; and its outward adornments vie with its internal acquirements in the beauty and variety of their tints. It has generally been thought to be a native of Barbary, although no proof can be adduced. They certainly are brought from Africa; and from the facility with which they bear a European climate, we may suppose the northern or mountainous districts are their native abodes.

The individual represented by F. Cuvier, and which has served for our copy, was procured to the Parisian Menagerie while very young, and on account of its mild and retiring manners was allowed to go at large. Age did not alter these traits of its character, and its gambols are performed with a sedate activity, which is not intrusive or disagreeable. Notwithstanding, its cunning and activity are very great, and particularly its adroitness in performing any little theft without the slightest noise. It will open a chest or drawer by turning the key in the lock, will untie knots, undo the rings of a chain, and will search one's pockets with a delicacy of touch which will not be felt until the theft has been discovered; the latter was its most favourite amusement, and a stranger seldom escaped without being rifled. It is playful when caressed, and will return them with gentleness, uttering at the time a low cry, as if an expression of pleasure, and in every way is free from the disgusting manners possessed by most other monkeys. Of their habits in a wild state, nothing whatever is known, and the account of those who have mentioned them can be reduced to no proof, and seem to be more the result of conjecture than of reality.

The colouring of a specimen in the Zoological Gardens is thus described by Mr Bennet, and appears the most correct we are acquainted with:—" The top of the head is of a greenish-yellow, mingled with a slight tinge of black, and the neck, back, and sides, are of a deep chestnut brown, passing downwards as far as the shoulders and haunches, where it changes into a dusky slate colour, which is continued on the limbs and tail. The latter organ is considerably longer than the body, and has, on each side of its base, a very remarkable white spot. The under surface of the body, and the inside of the limbs, are of a pure and delicate white, separated from the neighbouring colours by an abrupt line of demarcation.

" " The naked upper part of the face, comprehending the orbits and the cheeks, is of a bluish purple ; the lips, and so much of the chin as is without hair, flesh-coloured; on the sides of the face, large bushy whiskers, of a light straw colour, mixed with a few blackish rings, advance forwards, and cover a considerable portion of the cheeks. Above the eyebrows is a trans-verse black band, extending on each side as far as the ears, and surmounted by a narrow crescent-shaped stripe of gray, which is sometimes scarcely visible. The ears and the hands are of a livid flesh colour."

Another very beautiful allied species is the *Diana* or Palatine monkey, (*Cercopithecus Diana*, Geoff.,) so named by Linnæus from the white crescent-shaped band, the emblem of the Virgin Huntress, which adorns its brow.

It is a native of the eastern coast of Africa, principally in Guinea, is about eighteen inches in length, with a tail exceeding two feet. Its colouring. Mr

Bennet observes, is peculiarly varied and graceful.
The head, neck, sides, and middle of the body beneath,
are of a deep ash colour, gradually becoming darker
on the outside of the limbs, and finally changing into
a deep black upon the hands.　The tail also exhibits a
dark shade, and terminates with a point entirely black.
The general colour may be described as consisting of a
mixture of black and white, the former predominating,
and the whole having a grisly appearance.　But the most
conspicuous feature, is a straight line of long white hairs,
surmounting a less obvious one of black, which runs
in a crescent form across the forehead, above the eyes,
and extends nearly to the ears.　The specimen in
the Zoological Society was playful and familiar.　By
Linnæus the Diana monkey is said to be fond of all
kinds of vegetables, but particularly to delight in
fruits, raisins, nuts, and almonds; and would willingly
also eat eggs and bread, but animal food was not enjoyed; it drank often, and before taking anything
would always smell it.　It was remarkably fond of
heat; and, when the cold season commenced, gave
vent to its uneasiness in shrill complaints.　Every
thing that is set before the animal is turned over,
even the vessel which is put down with its food.
When a stranger is introduced it shows its teeth, and
bows repeatedly with the head · and, if enraged, endeavours to bite its enemy.

　　This genus will contain seven or eight species in
addition; for a brief notice of which we refer out

Stewart delt   Lizars sc.

CERCOPITHECUS RUBER.

(The Red Monkey)

readers to the note of species given at the conclusion.
We shall here only mention another animal, remarkable among its congeners for the uniformity of its
colouring, it is,

THE RED MONKEY.

Cercopithecus ruber.—Geoffroy.

Plate XI.

Simia rubra, *Linnæus.*—Cercopithecus ruber, *Geoffroy, Annales du Museum,* vol. xix. p. 96.—Guenon patas, *Desmarest's Mammalogie,* p. 59.—Le Patas, *Frederic Cuvier,
Histoire Naturelle des Mammiferes.*

It is a species long known, recorded so far back as
Prosper Alpinus, who has given both a figure and
description. The length of the body is about one foot
four or five inches, and that of the tail is nearly equal.
All the upper parts are of a brilliant reddish fawn
colour, which is shaded into a pale grayish tinge on
the arms and legs, and the face, cheeks, breast, and
belly, are pure white; a band of black hair crosses
above the eyebrows, and there are two lines of the
same colour upon the upper lip, in the shape of mus-
taches, which give the countenance a peculiar physiognomy. It is a native of Senegal. Mr. Bennet
mentions that a young individual in the Zoological
Museum, Bruton Street, "is lively and active, but

somewhat irascible when handled. When pleased, it dances on all-fours in a peculiar and measured step, which is far from being ungraceful, although after a time it becomes ludicrous from its regular monotony."

Two young specimens kept by F. Cuvier were mischievous at a very early age; and though not deficient in the penetration of their race, showed all the impatience and caprice which characterise the true Guenons.

In Geoffroy's second subdivision of the Guenons having the more elongated muzzle, and to which he has applied the title of *Cercocebus*, will be seen,

THE MANGABEY OR WHITE EYELID MONKEY.

Cercocebus fuliginosus.—GEOFFROY.

PLATE XII.

Simia ethiops, *Linnæus.*—White Eyelid Monkey, *Pennant's Quadrupeds*, 204.—Mangabey, *Buffon.*—Guenon enfumée, *Desmarest's Mammalogie*, p. 62 ; *Frederic Cuvier, Histoire Naturelle des Mammiferes.*—Cercocebus fuliginosus, *Geoffroy, Annales du Museum*, vol. xix. p. 97.

WE have placed this curiously-marked monkey first in this subdivision, as possessing considerable alliance in form to the preceding ; so much so, as to be by some zoologists placed with it. We prefer Geoffroy's

Stewart del.t   Lizars sc.

CERCOCEBUS FULIGINOSUS.

(The Mangabey or White-eyelid Monkey.)

arrangement, and look upon it as one of those con-
necting forms which can be so constantly traced.

Excepting the plate in Frederic Cuvier's *Mammiferes,* there is no good coloured representation of this
animal, and we were so fortunate as to procure a
drawing from a living female lately exhibited by Mr
Wombwell in Edinburgh.* This animal is generally
described to be mild and good-tempered, but very
restless and active; and the female we have alluded
to fully confirmed these accounts. She was certainly
a most lively animal, never for a moment at rest,
and particularly active when observed, as if conscious
of the notice she excited, and anxious to display her
talents. She performed many of the attitudes of the
most experienced Harlequins. When the sketch was
taken, she was particularly troublesome in her display,
and is represented in the attitude in which she most
frequently placed herself; sometimes extending the
one hand and sometimes the other. She was extremely
gentle, and never resented any of the troublesome
usage to which animals in a menagerie are so frequently subjected by their various visiters; on the contrary, she was delighted to see strangers, and seemed
flattered by their attentions. She was remarkably
cleanly and careful not to soil her person. When

* Mr Wombwell allowed Mr Lizars to make drawings from
several of the interesting animals in his collection, and the proprietor of the Naturalist's Library takes this opportunity to offer
his acknowledgments for Mr W.'s attentions.

M

feeding she seldom put her head to the food or dish, but lifted and conveyed it to her mouth. Her food was chiefly bread and milk, and occasionally vegetables, of which a carrot was a very favourite luxury.

This monkey is most appropriately named from the white colour of the eyelids, a most conspicuous feature in its physiognomy, and assisting the expression often thrown into the ridiculous grimaces, which, Mr Bennet remarks, " it continues in a state of confinement with laudable perseverance and unwearied zeal." In both this species and another, " the collared white eyelid monkey," (*Cercocebus ethiops*, Geoffroy,) the eyelids are of a very peculiar colour, a sort of clear grayish-white, but with a dead or chalky hue. In the female above alluded to, this colour was remarkably apparent, contrasting with the naked parts of the face, which resembled Indian rubber, and its transparent shade of dark brownish purple. The hair is fine and soft to the touch, and on the upper parts is of a dull sooty black (expressively named *enfumée* by the French naturalists,) darker upon the hands, gradually shading into a yellowish tint on the breasts, belly, and inside of the thighs. On these parts the thin coating of hair plainly showed the skin, which is very pure flesh-colour. The extremities are of the same colour and texture with the face ; and it has been remarked that they resembled a lady's hand covered with a very fine black kid glove.

The native country of the white eyelid monkey seems to be yet somewhat uncertain. The west coast of Africa is generally assigned to it; and the specimen which formed the subject of our plate, was said to be procured from that country.

The collared white eyelid monkey which we have mentioned, appears to inhabit the opposite or eastern side of the same continent, and is an animal of greater beauty. The upper part of the head is deep chestnut-brown, and the back of the neck is crossed by a collar of the purest white, which reaches forward upon the cheeks, and forcibly contrasts with the deep shade of the body.

Another animal placed in this division, and with what F. Cuvier terms the *Malbrouks*, may be almost said to join in a small group among the Guenons; they have a peculiarity of carrying the tail arched over the back, in the manner of a cur dog; and in parts of their form and physiognomy come much nearer to the baboons. The first we shall mention is

THE GREEN MONKEY.

Cercocebus sabœus.—GEOFFROY.

PLATE XIII.

St Jago monkey, *Edwards' Gleanings*, Plate 215.—The Green monkey, *Pennant's Quadrupeds*, 203.—Guenon callitriche, *Desmarest's Mammalogie*, page 61.—Cercocebus sabœus, *Geoffroy, Annales du Museum*, vol. xix. p. 99.—Le Callitriche, *Frederic Cuvier, Histoire Naturelle des Mammiferes.*

THE green monkey is one of the most abundant of this group, and is perhaps oftener seen in a captive state than any of the others. It is a native of the Cape Verd Islands and the continent of Africa, and in its disposition seems to possess part of the bad traits of the baboons, though it is at the same time lively and playful. That described by M. Cuvier, in the Menagerie du Museum, became very fierce and irascible, and even bit the keepers who happened to get within his reach.

The description given by Mr Bennet of the specimens in the Zoological Gardens, may be considered accurate; in some specimens, the shade of colouring varies, but there is no other variation of consequence.

CERCOCEBUS SABAUS.

(The Green Monkey.)

" The colour is greenish-yellow above, arising from
the ringing of the hairs with various shades of yellow
and black, but assumes more of a dark grizzled appearance on the sides of the body, and outer sides of the
limbs, which become gradually darker towards the
hands. The face, ears, and naked part of the hands, are
of a jet black; the former is of a triangular shape,
bounded above the eyes by a straight line of stiff black
hairs, and on the sides by spreading tufts of light hairs,
with a yellowish tinge, meeting in a point beneath the
chin. The neck and chest are white; the under parts of
the body have a yellowish tinge; and the inside of the
limbs is gray. The length of the head and body is
sixteen or eighteen inches, and that of the tail somewhat more."

This animal, or at least one under the title of the
" *Green Monkey*," has been mentioned by many travellers, who give accounts of the vast troops which
assemble together. In Adanson's Voyage to Senegal,
it is thus introduced :—

" But what struck me most, was the shooting of
monkeys, which I enjoyed within six leagues this side
of Podor, on the lands to the south of Donai, otherwise called Coq; and I do not think there ever was
better sport. The vessel being obliged to stay there
one morning, I went on shore, to divert myself with
my gun. The place was very woody, and full of
green monkeys, which I did not perceive but by their
breaking the boughs on the tops of the trees, from

whence they tumbled down upon me; for in other
respects they were so silent and nimble in their tricks,
that it would have been difficult to hear them. Here
I stopped, and killed two or three of them, before the
others seemed to be much frighted; however, when
they found themselves wounded, they began to look
for shelter, some by hiding themselves among the large
boughs, others by coming down upon the ground;
others, in fine, and these were the greatest number,
by jumping from one tree to another. Nothing could
be more entertaining, when several of them jumped
together on the same bough, than to see it bend under
them, and the hithermost to drop down to the ground,
while the rest got further on, and others were still
suspended in the air. As this game was going on, I
continued still to shoot at them; and though I killed
no less than three-and-twenty in less than an hour,
and within the space of twenty fathoms, yet not one
of them screeched the whole time, notwithstanding
that they united in companies, knit their brows
gnashed their teeth, and seemed as if they intended
to attack me."

Another species belonging to this group is Frederic Cuvier's *Malbrouk, Cercocebus cynosurus*, described and figured by that naturalist as an animal
of truly arboreal habits; walking with difficulty on
the ground, and exhibiting the greatest activity when
sporting on the bars of its cage; it could sustain itself

by successive darts from one side of its cage to the
other, performed by the force of its feet alone, and
would keep up this severe motion for a considerable
period.   When young it was docile and mild-tempered,
but age brought with it propensities more brutal.
The chief characteristic of its disposition, as it is in all
the congeners, is extreme caution, or, as it were, an
arrangement or previous plan of the actions to be
performed ; thus, in their attacks, the opportunity is
watched when the person or animal is off their guard
and otherwise employed, and it is always made from
behind ; wounds are inflicted with the teeth and
nails, and a sudden dart places them at a distance,
where they will remain, showing their anger with expressive changes of countenance, and watching the
time when the attack can be with safety renewed.

The countenance of this animal becomes more like
that of the baboons, and, with the feet and skin of the
ears, is black.   The cheeks, chin, and a band above the
eyes, are white, as also the under parts and the insides
of the legs ; all the other parts are of a yellowish-green,
and the general contour is so similar to the green monkey, that it has been mistaken for it in a young state.

Another allied animal, equally remarkable for the
beauty of its yellowish-green fur, is the red-vented
monkey, *Cercocebus pygerythrœus*—a native of the
forests to the interior of the Cape, truly arboreal, and
never met beyond the boundaries of the larger woody
tracts.   The form is somewhat different ; but the

similarity of the upper covering, tne white cheeks, and frontal band, place it close to those we have just now described.

We again refer to our Synopsis for an enumeration of the other *Cercocebi*, and will now proceed to the next forms, which will commence

THE BABOONS.

We have now reached these forms which conduct from monkeys of pleasing appearance and gentle manners, to the most disgusting of the whole tribe. They may be generally designated under the title of baboons, but naturally form themselves into two groups—those with the muzzle still more lengthened than the Guenons, but having the nostrils placed as it were on the face; a body of considerable size and strength, and the tail shorter; the dispositions becoming more sulky and untractable, furious and revengeful, when annoyed.* The second, comprised in the true *Cynocephali* of Cuvier, and which are at once characterised by the position of the nostrils at the very extremity of the muzzle. Their size is very large; their strength enormous; their dispositions possessing scarcely a good quality, and combining great fierceness and malignity, which, joined with their strength, renders them

* The vignette will give an idea of this form.

always dangerous in confinement or when attacked
in a wild state. The form and arrangement of the
teeth is nearly similar, except in size, among both
groups; the principal peculiarity will be observed in
the form of the canine teeth, which are of remarkable
strength. and in the grinders, the last of which has
an additional point, somewhat resembling that of
Semnopithecus.

The first genus to be mentioned is *Macacus* of
Lacepédè, into which we have also brought the *Rhesus*
monkey, retaining the two tail-less species by themselves. The *Ouanderou* has generally been taken
for the type of this form: but, before describing it,
we shall mention the *Macaque* of Frederick Cuvier,
(*Simia cynocephalus,* Linnæus), which evidently forms
the passage between the Guenons and Baboons. It
is distinguished by a blunt and elongated muzzle,
forming a facial angle of 40° to 45°; by the promi-
nency of the superciliary crests which cover the eyes,
and give a peculiar expression to the physiognomy,
and by the comparative shortness of the tail, which
is rarely equal to the length of the body.

In this species we still see the colouring of the
Guenons, and the length of tail is nearly equal to
that of the individuals we last described; but we
want the light and agile form, and see the proportions
heavily and strongly made. The head is large, the
muzzle short, the nose flat, and the superciliary ridges
ample and lowering; the fingers are united with a

membrane for the length of the first phalanx. The general position of the animal is on all-fours, or seated on its buttocks, and it generally feeds in one of these positions, either by the assistance of its hands, or by placing the muzzle at once among the food, always, however, filling the cheek-pouches, which are ample, before any portion has been swallowed. When asleep, it either lies on one side like a dog, or sits in a bent position, with the head reclining on the breast.

Monkeys have very seldom produced young in a state of confinement in this country, and they have been still more rarely brought to maturity. Frederic Cuvier gives an account of a pair of these animals which produced, though the young survived only a few days. The male and female were confined in separate cages, in sight of each other, and their demonstrations of the softer passions, induced their keepers to allow one habitation; nearly a year after the female proved with young, and in seven months gave birth to a female. It was well formed; the eyes were open at birth, and its nails were complete. It was however too weak to support itself, and the mother treated it with no attention, did not attempt to suckle it, and entirely left it; the next day it died. Some time after, a second female was produced, under similar circumstances, and all attempts to rear it were equally unsuccessful.

Another monkey, which ought to stand in this place, is the *Toque* of Frederic Cuvier, *Macacus sinicus*.

PLATE 14

Stewart delt.   Lizars sc.

MACACUS SILENUS.

(The Wanderoo Monkey.

It is remarkable for the slender form of the muzzle, but approaches nearer to *Cercocebus* in colouring, and has a longer tail than the generality of our present group.

We have now endeavoured to represent,

THE WANDEROO MONKEY.

Macacus silenus.—LACEPEDE.

PLATE XIV.

Lion-tailed baboon, *Pennant's Quadrupeds*, 198.—Macaque à criniere, *Cuvier, Regne Animal*, i. 95; *Audibert, Histoire Naturelle des Singes.*—Papio silenus, *Geoffroy, Annales du Museum*, vol. xix. p. 102.—The Wanderoo monkey, *Gardens and Menagerie of the Zoological Society*, p. 21.

THE Wanderoo, or lion-tailed monkey of Pennant, is so well marked, that a description, in addition to the figure, is almost unnecessary.

Knox describes it shortly and quaintly in his Ceylon: He says, " there are abundance in the woods, as large as English spaniel dogs, of a darkish-gray colour, and black faces, with great white beards round from ear to ear, which make them show just like old men. They do little mischief, keeping in the woods, eating only leaves and buds of trees; but when they are catched they will eat anything. This sort they call, in their language, *Wanderows.*"

A specimen in the collection of the Zoological Society is extremely active, and occasionally troublesome, but is good-tempered; he is, however, yet young, and may afterwards prove dangerous from his strength. " His favourite exercise appears to consist in throwing himself together, with his chain over the transverse bar, which passes from pole to pole, and swinging himself backwards and forwards, while thus suspended by his loins. When a party enters the room, he usually descends his pole with rapidity, and watches a favourable opportunity for jumping upon some of them unawares, and carrying off a hat, or whatever else he may happen to seize, with which he instantly reascends his pole, and seats himself at the top, enjoying the success of his scheme." *

In some of the other species the tail becomes much shorter, such as the *M. rhœsus* and *nemestrina;* but a better idea will be formed from the vignette on the titlepage.

We shall proceed to the next genus, *Inuus* of Cuvier, and have given, as an illustration,

* Gardens of Menagerie.

Stewart del.   Lizars sc.

INUUS SYLVANUS.

[The Barbary Ape.]

THE BARBARY APE.

Inuus sylvanus.—CUVIER.

PLATE XV.

Simia inuus, *Linnæus.*—Magot, *Buffon; Frederic Cuvier,
Histoire Naturelle des Mammiferes.*—Macaque magot, *Des_
marest's Mammalogie,* p. 67.—Barbary ape, *Pennant's
Quadrupeds; Gardens of Zoological Society.*—Magot Afri-
cain, Inuus ecudatus, *Geoffroy, Annales du Museum,* xix.
p. 100.

THIS monkey is remarkable, both on account of its
peculiar form, and as being the only quadrumanous
animal found on the European continent. By Frederic Cuvier it is thought to be limited in its geographical distribution to Barbary and Egypt, and
the southern districts of Spain, and not to extend
over Africa to China and India, as some naturalists
allege. But the most celebrated abode of this species
is the precipitous sides of the rock of Gibraltar, which
is said by a historian of its celebrated siege to be remarkable for the number of apes about its summit,
breeding in inaccessible places, and appearing in large
droves with their young on their backs, on the western face of the hill.

Frederic Cuvier says, that they walk most commonly on all-fours, while at the same time they are very active climbers. He confirms the opinion of them being gregarious, filling the forests with their vast troops, and openly attacking those enemies which they think they can overcome, while they drive to a distance, by their numbers and screaming an intruder of whose powers they are doubtful. In a state of captivity it is capable of more than ordinary powers of comprehension; but, to improve those abilities as far as possible, it should be procured young, as with advanced age they generally become more sullen and morose, and even sometimes dangerous. It is very frequently seen at home, and, next to the green monkey, has the misfortune to be most frequently selected to accompany strolling bands, and owes most of its torments to the superior intelligence it is endowed with.

In captivity, it agrees with fruits, bread, and boiled vegetables, particularly carrots and potatoes; and its natural gregarious dispositions appear also to be preserved in its delighting in the society of some little animal, which is often placed in its company. Our plate from Frederic Cuvier will give an idea of its form and appearance. The females are nearly similar, though generally less in size.

There is another tail-less animal which we would introduce in this place, as forming the real passage to the true *Cynocephali*. It is the *Cynocephalus niger*

of Cuvier; while the modern British zoologists
place it in company with the Barbary ape and the
Rhæsus monkey. The general resemblance and physiognomy ally it to the dog-faced baboons, which is
strengthened by the swelled cheeks and flat nose;
but the position of the nostrils, with habits characteristic of the *Macaci*, and the total want of any
tail, join it with the preceding. Four specimens
only seem yet to be known; one in the Royal
Museum in Paris; another in the Tower of London,
described by Mr Grey in his Spicelogia Zoologica;
another more lately exhibited in Exeter Change, and
the fourth in the London Zoological Gardens, which
is thus described by Mr Bennet:—

"Our animal is of a deep jet black in all its parts,
with the exception of its large callosities, which are
flesh-coloured. The body is covered with long woolly
hair, becoming shorter on the limbs; its ears are small;
its tail a mere tubercle, less than an inch in length;
and its cheek-pouches seem to be capable of much
distension. Its face is broad, rather prominent, slightly
narrowing at the muzzle, and abruptly truncate, with
the nostrils placed very obliquely on the upper surface. On the top of the head it has a broad tuft of
long hairs, falling backwards, and forming a very remarkable crest. The expression of its physiognomy
is peculiarly cunning. It seems to be rather violent
in its temper, and tyrannizes not a little over the quiet

gray Gibbon, which is at present confined in the same cage."

The native country of this monkey is yet somewhat uncertain; but the best authorities record it as the islands of the Indian Archipelago.

With this species we close what was mentioned as the first division of the Baboons, and enter upon the second—the *Cynocephali* of Cuvier. These, according to the researches of the brother of this great naturalist, consist of only six species, which are again subdivided into two very natural sections. The one, with a considerable length of tail; the other, with the muzzle swollen upon the sides, and in the adults raised into coloured ridges, while the tail is a tubercle finished by a tuft of hairs, and stands erect, appearing, from the position of the coccyx, as if placed upon the lower part of the back itself.

The *Cynocephali* are all of large size, and indeed exceed that of any of the quadrumanæ, if we except the adult orang-outang; their proportions combine strength and activity, and their physiognomy fierceness with intelligence; while their dispositions are so fickle, or so easily affected—the transition from one passion to another is so rapid, that they are never to be trusted—and the paroxysms of their rage are described by F. Cuvier to be so great, that some have fallen victims to the consequences. That zoologist thinks that in this group the active animal passions are developed

to their utmost extent. In a wild state, they possess
an intuitive knowledge of what will harm them,
and combining with it great cunning, they most
frequently disappoint their enemies. They attack at
a distance, and threaten with their cries, but only
use their powerful strength, and formidable tusks, when
compelled by danger. The naturalist we have mentioned above, would even attribute to them a power
of higher intelligence—that they will destroy a planta-
tion from revenge, watching their opportunity; and
he relates an anecdote of the Chacma,* which severely
bit his keeper upon being threatened to be struck,
though the animal had never seen a stick, and had
never been beaten. In like manner, he continues,
are these animals so susceptible of the instruction of
circumstances in a wild state, capable of receiving it
artificially from man, and they are often met with
performing various feats at the command of their
keepers; but he adds, it is only when young that they
thus submit. They retain a kind of docility longer
than the period of their youth, but it is effected in a
different way; their passions or their likings must
be administered to. Such was the case with the specimen of the Mandril so long exhibited in Exeter Change,
under the name of " Happy Jerry." He would have
done anything for gin and water, and the love of drink
became so strong, that he would have made any

* See description, page 156.

N

sacrifice: perhaps some theorists will adduce this common vice as an argument for the common nature of men and monkeys. We have heard of another animal of this kind, possessed of a curious propensity, which might serve as an additional proof towards the same end; he was kept at large by a gentleman, who kept also a pack of harriers, and to enjoy either the noise or the sport, would travel to an eminence whenever the hounds threw off. This love for field-sports had, however, nearly proved fatal. The hounds one day got upon Jerry's trail on his return home, and he was only saved by a tree occurring opportunely. Superior intelligence was, on this occasion, so far displayed, that Jerry never afterwards enjoyed hare hunting.

These baboons having the general organization of the quadrumanous animals, are necessarily arboreal in their habits, though not to such an extent as the other monkeys of the Old World; and they are at greater ease when on the ground, on account of the more accurate proportion of the hind quarters, though their motions there are still awkward and constrained. Their pace is generally a kind of slow gallop, performed by alternate undulations of the whole fore and hinder parts. Their agility on a tree is, however, surprising when we look at their heavy bodies; they possess all the power of grasping and swinging; take immense leaps, and will in a manner tumble from one part of a tree to another, before the spectator can think

PAPIO SALVANUS.
The Chacma.

it possible. In this way they equally possess qualifications for pursuing or eluding an enemy. They feed chiefly on fruits and roots, or the young and tender shoots of
various plants. Their natural country is the warmer
parts of Africa and India. They are very susceptible of cold, and great care has to be taken with those
kept in confinement in Europe, and, even with every
precaution, a few years is generally the limit of their
existence. The hair is longer than usual, and forms
a sort of mane on the upper parts.

For an illustration of the first form among the
Cynocephali, we have selected,

THE CHACMA.

Papio comatus.—GEOFFROY.

PLATE XVI.

Babuin chevelu, Papio comatus, *Geoffroy, Annales du Museum*,
xix. p.103.—Cynocephalus chacma, *Desmarest's Mammalogie*,
p. 69.—Le Chacma, *Frederic Cuvier's Histoire Naturelle
des Mammiferes.*

THE animal which formed the subject of the annexed plate, copied from that in the Histoire Naturelle
des Mammiferes, was procured very young. During
his youth his frolics made him amusing, but his mischievous disposition soon became dangerous, and it

became necessary to chain him at the door of a court. There he performed the office of a watch-dog, and very soon became the terror even of his keepers. From his ferocity, his master was obliged to get rid of him.

F. Cuvier relates another instance of ferocity in a specimen kept in the Jardin du Roi. This animal made his escape from his cage to the enclosure in which he was confined. His keeper imprudently threatened him with a stick, which so enraged the animal that he darted upon him, and before the man's release could be affected, wounded him so severely on the thigh as to put his life in danger. Nor could every endeavour prevail on the animal to return to his confinement, until his rage was again roused by the following expedient. The keeper's daughter often supplied him with food, and seemed a great favourite. She placed herself at a door opposite that of the cage through which the animal had to pass, and a stranger appearing to caress her, the chacma darted upon him, but was secured before he could pass through his cage.

The *Chacma* is a native of Africa, in the neighbourhood of the Cape of Good Hope. The colour is of a greenish or grayish-black, paler upon the fore part of the shoulders and flanks. The neck is clothed with long hair, in the form of a mane, which has furnished Geoffroy with a character for the name he has attached. The skin of the face and extremities are of a purplish-black, relieved around the eyes by a paler

tint, and by the upper eyelids, which are nearly
white, as in the mangabey or white eyelid monkey.
It is also remarkable in having the naked callosities
very small.

Another animal allied in colour is the dog-faced
baboon of Pennant, the *Tartarin* of F. Cuvier, thought
originally to be a native of Arabia, but at present
rare in the European collections. It is equally fierce
and dangerous with the preceding; of a greenish-gray
colour; the anterior part of the body clothed with
very long and shaggy hair.

The next animals we shall mention are *Le Babouin*
and *Le Papion* of Frederic Cuvier. The first, apparently, is the *Simia cynocephalus* of Linnæus, and is
thought by the above-mentioned author to be one of
those adored in the temple of Hermopolis, and so frequently seen among the Egyptian hieroglyphics.

The colour is of a uniform yellowish-green, paler on
the under parts; and the more remarkable deviations
of form, are in the nostrils being prolonged to the
length of the jaws, separated above by a very marked
hollow, and by the lateral cartilages advancing as far
forward as that in the centre. The tail is raised at
its origin, and appears as if placed in the same position with that of the *Mandril*, but is of considerable
length, reaching below the hams. It may be remarked, that this baboon has been confounded with
the next, which Frederic Cuvier considers perfectly
distinct and has named *Le Papion*. This animal is

considerably larger in size; the colour is of a ruddier hue; the cartilages of the nose are longer than the jaws; and the colour of the skin on the face, extremities, and ears, are black, while the upper eyelids are white. It is a native of Africa, but hitherto undescribed by any traveller in a state of nature.

To illustrate the second form of the true *Cynocephali,* we have figured,

THE MANDRIL OR RIB-NOSE BABOON.

Papio mormon.—GEOFFROY.

PLATE XVII.

Ribbed-nose baboon, *Pennant's Quadrupeds,* p. 190.—*Papio mormon, Geoffroy, Annales du Museum,* xix. p. 184.— Cynocephalus mandril, *Desmarest's Mammalogie,* p. 70.—Le Mandril, *Frederic Cuvier, Histoire Naturelle des Mammiferes; Audibert, Histoire Naturelle des Singes.*

THIS formidable animal, the fiercest and most powerful of its race, is a native of the Guinea Coast, and has been well known for a long period in our menageries. In an adult state, the colours of its fur may vie with any of the quadrumanæ, and the general effect is heightened at a little distance by the rich blue and purple shades of the muzzle, lips, and other naked parts of the skin. Upon a nearer view, however, these beauties do not compensate for its other-

PAPIO MORMON

(The Mandrel or Rib-nose Baboon)

wise disgusting appearance. A representation has been given of this animal;* and it may be remarked, that it is only in the adults where the brilliancy of the colouring is observed. In the young, the hair is of a uniform tawny-green, paler underneath and inside the legs, and assuming a yellowish tinge on the cheeks; the ridges upon the muzzle commence to appear of a livid blue, and the bright red of the nose and lips is of a dull flesh colour. The females are less in size, and the colouring of the naked parts is never so vivid.

"Happy Jerry," the property of Mr. Cross, and so long the prominent attraction to Exeter Change, was a ribbed-nose baboon. He is described to have been docile to his keepers, but easily exasperated by strangers; and among other accomplishments, had been taught to drink *sling* and smoke *tobacco*. In the first he delighted; but I rather think the latter was not such a favourite, and a bribe of gin and water was generally promised before his performance. His cage was furnished with a small but strong arm-chair, into which, when ordered, he would seat himself with great gravity and await further orders. All his manœuvres were performed with great slowness and composure. His keeper having lighted the pipe, presented it to him; he inspected it minutely, sometimes feeling it with his finger, as if to know if lighted, before in-

* From the plate in Cuvier's Menagerie du Museum.

serting it in his mouth. It was then introduced almost
up to the bowl, but with that part generally downwards, and it was retained without any appearance of smoke for some minutes, during which time
the animal completely filled his cheek-pouches and
capacious mouth, and would then exhale a volume,
filling his cage from mouth, nose, and sometimes even
the ears. He generally finished with gin and water,
which was handed to him in a goblet ; this he grasped
in one hand, and was not long in discussing.

He was possessed of enormous strength. Two men
could with difficulty withdraw the end of a rope he
one day seized, though they were assisted by the resistance of their feet upon the base of his cage.

He was fed chiefly on vegetables, and preferred
them cooked ; but when he visited Windsor, where
he was exhibited to his late Majesty, he is said to
have dined upon hashed venison with no ordinary
degree of avidity.

The only other animal belonging to this group which
we shall mention, is one which was long involved in
obscurity, and whose young state was frequently
confounded with that we have now described ; it is,

PAVIO LEUCOPHÆUS

The Drill.

THE DRILL.

Papio leucophæus.—F. CUVIER.

PLATE XVIII.

Le Drill, *Frederic Cuvier, Histoire Naturelle des Mammiferes.*—Cynocèphale drill, Cynocephalus leucophæus, *Desmarest's Mammalogie*, p. 71.

THE *Drill* is nearly as strong and powerful as the
Mandril, and has a similar form. The colours of
the adult are also nearly alike, generally of a duller
hue; but the principal distinguishing character is the
absence of the ridges upon the muzzle, and of bright
colouring except the border of the upper lip, which,
by Fred. Cuvier, is represented of a bright red.
The under parts are also white. The female
differs in a less size and duller colouring, and by the
head being of a shorter proportion. The native
country seems somewhat uncertain, but it most probably is also Africa.

With these animals, the forms of the Old World
terminate; and we now commence the second great
geographical division of the quadrumanæ.

THE MONKEYS OF SOUTH AMERICA;
THOSE OF THE NEW WORLD.

THE forms contained in this division are almost entirely confined to the tropical regions of the Southern Continent.*   They differ in a remarkable degree from all those we have described in the previous part of this volume, and in no instance can the South American species be classed with the inhabitants of the Indian or African Continents.   The most striking outward differences, are the smaller size and less ferocious manners of the greater number, the prehensile tail of many, and the want in all of the cheek-pouches and naked callosities.   Internally, the larynx is re-markable for its great developement, and the teeth are thirty-six instead of thirty-two, and, besides, differ considerably in their structure, as will be perceived in the woodcuts we have introduced.

In the arrangement of this geographical group, we have followed that of Geoffroy Saint Hilaire, with the exception of placing the howlers (*Mycetes*) first, as the

* Named *Platyrrhini* by Geoffroy.

Baron Cuvier has done, instead of *Ateles*, and of following them by that genus, and *Cebus* of Xerleben.

THE HOWLERS

contain a single genus, named by Illiger *Mycetes*,[*]
from the remarkable howling voice of the animals. It
is characterised by a facial angle of about 30° ; the
tail very long, naked at the extremity, and prehensile.
·The dentition, according to Frederic Cuvier, is nearly
similar in this and the two next genera ; and we add
the delineation which he considers typical of these

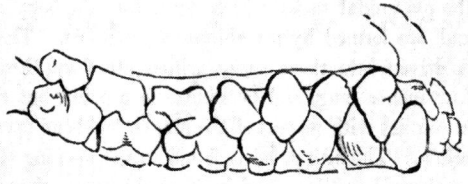

forms. But the prominent character in this group is
the extraordinary developement of the larynx, which is
ventricose, and appears on the outside in the form of

* Μυκητης howling.

a swelling. The internal structure of this member, in the *Mono colorado* of Humboldt, is thus described in his Zoological Observations, and will serve as a model for the others. " The bony case of the os hyoides, measured by water, gave a size equal to four cubic inches; the larynx was slightly attached by muscular fibres, and communicated by a membranous canal. The larynx consisted of six pouches of ten lines in length, to from three to five in depth. These pouches resemble those of the small whistling monkeys, squirrels, and some birds. They have an opening above on the same side with that of the glottis, by which the air cannot enter without shutting the epiglottis. Above the pouches there are two others, of which the lips or borders are yellowish. These are the pyramidal sacks which enter into the bony case, and are formed by membranous partitions. The air is driven into these sacks, which are from three to four inches long, and terminate in a point, but come in contact with no part of the large hyoid bone opening below. The fifth pouch is found in the opening of the arythenoid cartilage, and is situated between the pyramidal sacks of the same form, but shorter; and the sixth pouch is formed by the bony drum itself, within which the voice acquires the mournful and plaintive tone which characterises these animals."* The

* Humboldt, Zool. Observ. I. p. 9.

annexed cut, from Humboldt, will show the form of
the drum of the os hyoides.

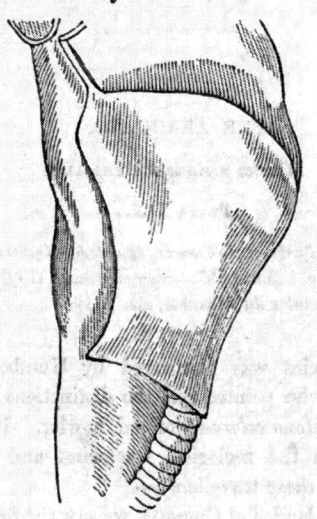

The howlers are also the largest of the American
monkeys; in their disposition, and fierce manners,
and declination of the facial angle, they may be said
to represent the Baboons of the Old World, while, in
the nightly howlings and gregarious habits, they bear
some analogy to the Gibbons. The form of this genus
will be seen in

THE ARAGUATO.

Mycetes ursinus.—HUMBOLDT.

PLATE XIX.

Simia ursina, L'araguata de Caracas, *Humboldt, Observations de Zoologie,* i. p. 329 and 355.—Stentor ursinus, *Geoffroy Saint Hilaire, Annales du Museum,* xix. p. 108.

THIS species was discovered by Humboldt and Bonpland, who pointed out the distinctions between it and the *Mono colorado,* or red howler. It is thus described in the zoological researches and personal narrative of these travellers :—

" Having landed at Cumana, we saw the first troops of Araguatos in our journey to the mountains of Cocallor and cavern of Guacharo; and although the convent of Carisse is situated at a high elevation, and the degree of cold during the night considerable,* the surrounding forests abound with the *Araguatos,* whose mournful howling is heard at the distance of half a league, especially when the weather is open, or the

* Centigrade Thermometer fell to 70°.

MYCETES URSINUS.

(The Araguato.)

e.ectric state of the air foretels rain or a storm. We have met with them also in the valleys of Aragua, upon the Llanos of the Apure and Lower Oronooko, and in the missions of the Caribes in the province of New Barcelona, but in greatest abundance near the pools of stagnant water, shaded by the *Mauritia flexuosa*."

They feed on fruit as well as the leaves of vegetables. The females are often seen carrying the young upon the shoulder; but no difference in the colour between the ages or sexes was ever perceived. Humboldt thinks, of all gregarious monkeys, none appear so numerous as this species: upon the banks of the Apure he has counted above forty upon one tree; and he has no doubt, that upon a square league of these wild countries, above two thousand may be found.

"The eye, voice, and gait, denote melancholy. I have seen young *Araguatoes* brought up in the Indian huts, which never play like the *Sagoins;* and their gravity was described with much simplicity by Lopez de Gomara in the beginning of the sixteenth century. 'The *Araguata de los cumanenses*,' says this author, ' has the face of a man, the beard of a goat, and a grave behaviour.' "*

The *Araguato* has something the appearance of a young bear; it is nearly three feet in length indepen-

* Personal Narrative, iii. p. 172.

dent of the tail, and is entirely covered with a thick reddish fur. It is distinguished from the *Mono colorado* by the longer hair upon the body, the less bushy beard, and by the under parts being clothed with hair of the same colour with the other parts. and not of the brownish black which the naked skin of the Red Howler exhibits. They differ also in their gait, and in the sound of their voice.

The fruit, which it is represented eating, is that of the *Inga vera*, Wildenow.

Another singular species was discovered by Humboldt—the *Mycetes flavicauda*, and is described by him under the name of " *Le choro de lo provence a Jaen.*" It inhabits the banks of the river Amazon, in the provinces of Jaen and Maynas. The colour is a brown, shading to black, and dullest on the lower parts ; the face yellowish-brown ; the tail, shorter than the body, is the most characteristic mark, and is greenish-black. adorned upon the sides with two yellowish stripes, an anomalous distribution of colour among this family. The hair is very long, soft and shining, and the skin forms an object of commerce among the natives; it is also used by them to cover seats, and for the saddle-cloths of the mules on which the periodical journey to the Cordilleras is made.

The other animals which constitute this group are only seven in number, and inhabit the western provinces, where abundance of wood is essentially necessary for them. They are gregarious, and generally

very abundant, and in all the sonorous voice is conspicuous.

The next group which occurs is

THE SAPAJOUS,

Containing animals of a more slender form; milder
dispositions; the face rather flat; the tail very long,
and the whole form in the general contour allied to
the Guenons of the Old World. The first genus to be
mentioned is *Ateles* of Geoffroy, so named from the
imperfect structure of the fore extremities, which want
the thumbs, and thus bear analogy to those of *Colobus*
in the first geographical division. It may be characterised by a facial angle of about 60°; by the extremities being very long and slender; the fore
hands destitute of a thumb, or having that member
supplied by a rudiment; the tail very long, covered
at the tip with a delicate skin, strongly prehensile;
the os hyoides large, but not apparent on the outside.

By Geoffroy, two species, which have a rudimentary
thumb, are generally placed at the commencement of
this genus—the *A. hypoxanthus* and *Subpentadactylus;*
but the form is well represented by

THE COAITA.

Ateles paniscus. —GEOFFROY.

PLATE XX.

Simia paniscus, *Linnæus.* — Coaita, *Buffon.* — Four-fingered monkey, *Pennant.*—Ateles paniscus, *Geoffroy Saint Hilaire, Annales du Museum,* xix. p. 105 ; *Desmarest, Mammalogie,* p. 73 ; *Humboldt, Observations de Zoologie,* i. p. 352.—Le Coaita, *Frederic Cuvier, Histoire Naturelle des Mammi-feres.*

THIS curious monkey, apparently possessing all the exterior necessaries for great activity, is nevertheless, Frederic Cuvier remarks, one of the most sluggish. It moves with slowness, and, as it were, with a dragging motion. The limbs are placed in the necessary posi-tions with deliberation, and as if every movement required a fresh exercise of thought to determine their position. The tail is constantly made use of, and is never relieved from one object until the feet are firmly fixed, when it is again wound round some other object of support, as if the former were not sufficiently capa-ble to maintain it.

The animal described by Cuvier, and from which

ATELES PANISCUS.
(The Coaita.)

Stewart del.

Scott sc.

our illustration is taken, was a female, at that
period young, and joined to a considerable degree of
intelligence a mild and affectionate disposition. The
body is covered with long soft and silky, but strong
black hair, thinner on the under parts, and without
any mixture of a woolly texture. The fore extremities
want the thumb; the hinder are formed like the other
quadrumanæ, but with longer fingers; and the long
prehensile tail is terminated on the under side with a
tender and fine skin, which seems to be endowed, like
the hands, with the sense of touch. It makes use of
it to grasp any object of support, suspends itself, and
uses it to draw towards it any objects which are beyond the reach of its hands. F. Cuvier says they are
met with in large troops in the forests of Guiana and
Brasil; but Humboldt says, that in all his extensive
travels he has never met with the true *Ateles panis-*
cus, and that the most common species on the Cassi-
quiare and High Oronooko is the next animal we shall
mention, the *Ateles Belzebub* of Geoffroy, and the
Marimonda of Humboldt and Bonpland. These
naturalists describe it as also very slow in its movements, mild but timid in disposition; in the excess of
terror even biting those who caress it, and venting
its temporary rage in a guttural cry of ou-ó. Among
all the monkeys with prehensile tails, Humboldt thinks
that this species possesses the most perfect use and
sensibility of it; it can even, without turning its
head, introduce it into narrow chinks or rents, and

hook out any substance.* He has never observed the species use it, however, to convey food or any article to the mouth. They inhabit the banks of the Oronooko in immense numbers, and are often seen suspended from the trees, hanging to each other by tail and hands, in the most grotesque groups. At another time, these travellers would see them, under the most scorching sun, throw back their head, fold their arms upon their backs, and, raising their eyes to the sky, remain in this position for several hours.

The hair of the *Marimonda* is very long and shining upon the upper parts; on the under parts of a yellow-ish-red, shining in the sun with a golden lustre. The direction of the hair upon the head is remarkable; that on the hinder part and crown grows forward, while that of the forehead is directed backwards, and the meeting or opposition of the hairs forms a tuft, which does not improve the physiognomy of the animal; the face is naked and black, the mouth surrounded with pale-coloured hairs; the lips are capable of considerable extension forward, and the end of the nose is of a reddish-white—altogether, a combination irreconcilable to pleasing expression.

It is a remarkable circumstance that, among the South American Indians, monkeys are much more frequently used as food than among the inhabitants of

---

* The natives assert that it fishes also with the end of this prehensile organ!

the Old World, and on the Oronooko the broiled limbs
of the *Marimonda* were frequently seen by Humboldt
in the huts of the natives; and at Emeralda he examined roasted and dried bodies in an Indian hut,
which were prepared for an annual harvest fete.*

Another curious animal belonging to this group is
the *Chuva* of Humboldt, (*Ateles marginatus*, Geoffroy.)
inhabiting the province of Jaen de Bracamoros on the
river of the Amazons, where they live also in troops, but
always separate from the *Marimonda*. It resembles
that animal in its manners, but is distinguished by
the larger size and deep black colour of the upper
parts, and in the breast and inner sides of the legs
and arms only being white.

The next form occurring, is named by Geoffroy
Lagothrix; and we regret that we have been unable
to procure any illustration of it. The genus may be
characterised by a facial angle of 50°. The head
rounder than in the last; hands provided with thumbs;
the tail long and prehensile, naked at the tip underneath; the os hyoides outwardly apparent; the hair
rough and curled. Two species only are yet discovered; the one mentioned by Geoffroy and Desmarest, but

* A French writer, speaking of monkeys as a *dish,* says, " The
are excellent eating, and that a ' *soupe aux singes*' will be found
as good as any other, as soon as you have conquered the aversion
to the *bouilli* of their heads, which look very like those of little
children."

yet imperfectly known ; said to inhabit Brasil ; of a grayish ash colour, with reddish head, hands, and tail. The other, discovered by Humboldt and described by him under the name of *Caparro*, has been dedicated by Geoffroy to that naturalist, and will stand in our systems as *Lagothrix Humboldtii.*   It inhabits the banks of the Guaviaré, one of the tributaries of the Oronooko, where it was discovered by Humboldt and Bonpland, in the hut of an Indian, who had taken it in an excursion to the west.   It is an animal of considerable size, being about two feet two inches in length, exclusive of the tail.   The head is round, and singularly large.   The hair is long, strong, and uniformly of a martin gray ; having the tips black.   The face is naked and black, but the mouth is surrounded by long and stiff bristles.   The tail, slightly longer than the body, is prehensile, and naked at the extremity.   They live in numerous bands, and are frequently seen, says Humboldt, raised upon the hinder extremities.   We are not aware of a specimen of this animal in any of the collections in this country.

We must now describe another form, included in the genus *Cebus* of Xerleben.   The animals contained in this genus, exhibit great activity ; are excellent climbers, and in all their members show great adaptation for a silvan life.   The fore hands are very perfectly formed, more so than those of the monkeys of the Old Continent, and

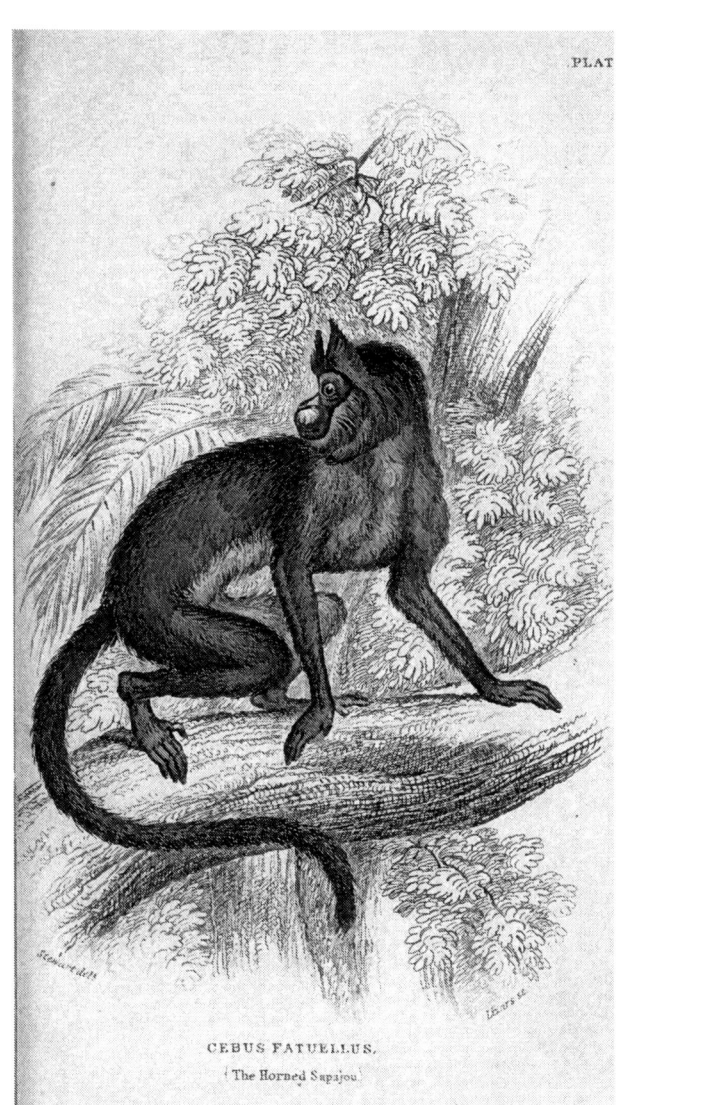

CEBUS FATUELLUS.

(The Horned Sapajou)

the thumb bears a better proportion, from its greater length; the palms of both fore and hinder extremities are very sensible of touch. The general size is small, the dispositions mild and playful; the food chiefly fruit and insects; they are gregarious, and, generally speaking, they may be said to supply the place of the Guenons of the Old World. They embrace all the remaining monkeys of the New World, which are possessed of prehensile tails.

The characters of this genus are, a facial angle of about 60°; head round, and the muzzle short; the tail prehensile, and entirely covered with hair. The first species we shall mention is,

THE HORNED SAPAJOU.

Cebus fatuellus.—GEOFFROY.

PLATE XXI.

Simia fatuellus, *Linnæus.*—Sajou cornu, Cebus fatuellus, *Geoffroy Saint Hilaire, Annales du Museum,* xix. p. 109; *Desmarest's Mammalogie,* p. 84.—Le Sajou cornu male, et variete, *Frederic Cuvier, Histoire Naturelle des Mammiferes.*

THIS Sapajou, of grotesque figure, from the unusual direction of the hair upon the forehead, in general form, will show the proportions of this genus. It has been long known, and was established in the

Systema Naturæ of Linnæus, from specimens described by Brisson.

The general colour of those figured by Frederic Cuvier, is a very deep brownish-black, while the specimens which Buffon and Audibert represent, are rather of a reddish-brown. We have copied the figures from Cuvier, being taken from living specimens, and they may be considered as the most correct plates of the adult state of this animal. The *Horned Sapajou* is one of the largest in the family ; all the upper parts are very deep purplish or brownish-black, nearly black on the head and upon the shoulders, and the dark purple of the skin, which appears on the naked parts, gives a uniformity of shade to the whole. The grotesque figure of the head is covered by the hair of the front, which stands erect, in a curved or crescent form, and, when viewed in front, has the appearance of two horns ; the tips of these hairs, and those on the cheeks, are of a paler shade. A variety which Cuvier figures has a greater portion of white about the tufts and-jaw.

Geoffroy and Desmarest give French Guiana as the native country of this species.

The most common species of *Sapajou*, and that which is most frequently seen in this country, is the Weeper monkey, *Cebus appella* of zoologists. It recommends itself for confinement by its good temper, playful disposition, and hardy constitution. It is also of a small size ; and, though not clothed in a fur of rich colour, it is of a chaste and pleasing tinge, and, when the animal is healthy, of a shining, soft and silky texture. The shades are generally a sort of olive, tinged with a golden yellow on the light parts ; the face is surrounded with a circle of paler colours, which varies considerably in its shade and breadth, being in some nearly wanting. This has given rise to several species being formed from it, and to some confusion in its alliance to one or two other Sapajous ; and, indeed, Humboldt seems almost of opinion, that the animal we have just now figured is only a variety of this. Some have been known to produce young ones in confinement.

Another allied species, described by the last-mentioned naturalist, is the *Ouavapavi des cataractes—Cebus albifrons.* It is about the same size, the colour of the face grayish-blue, except the orbits and front, which are pure white ; and the contrast thus exhibited, at once distinguishes it from those above noticed. The general colour of the body is grayish-olive, lighter on the back and belly. Humboldt met with this animal in troops in the forests near the cataracts of the Oronooko, and the mission of Santa Barbara. They are extremely mild in disposition, and very active ; often kept by the Indians, and one was seen by Humboldt, at Maypures, which every morning caught a pig, and continued seated on his back during the day, while feeding in the savanna round the Indian huts. Another is mentioned, in the house of a missionary, which would often ride upon a cat, which had been reared in its company, and which patiently suffered the exploits of the *Ouavapavi.*

Like the Guenons of the Old Continent, the Sapajous are the most numerous group in America; fifteen or sixteen species seem to be well established, and are enumerated in our Synopsis. We shall only describe another in this place, which is remarkable chiefly for the great proportional size of the head. It is,

THE LARGE-HEADED SAPAJOU.

Cebus monachus.—F. Cuvier.

Plate XXII.

Le saï à grosse tête, mâle; Cebus monachus, *Frederic Cuvier, Histoire Naturelle des Mammiferes.*

The most striking feature in this animal is the size of the head; and the effect is heightened by the short or shorn-like white hairs which cover it; the breast and belly, sides of the cheeks, and whole front before the arms, are yellowish-white; the fore-arms, posterior extremities, and tail, are black; and a mixture of black and brown, disposed in irregular patches, covers the back and rest of the body. F. Cuvier was ignorant from what part of America his specimen was received.

CEBUS MONACHUS
The Large-headed Sapajou.

We now come to another form, which, though joined by many zoologists with the preceding, presents very considerable differences in form and habits. We begin to enter with it those small species where the nails take the form of claws, and where the habits become more akin to the little carnivora; raw meat, insects, and birds are relished by them, and the latter are taken with great activity. The nearest in alliance to the Sapajous is the genus *Callithrix* of Geoffroy characterised by a facial angle of 60°; ears proportionally very large; the body slender; the tail longer than the body, entirely hairy, but not prehensile; the nails straight and raised; colours of the fur bright. The type of the genus has been taken by Geoffroy in the *Simia sciurea* of Linnæus, which should now stand as

THE SIAMIRI.

Callithrix sciureus.—GEOFFROY.

PLATE XXIII.

Simia sciurea, *Linnæus.*—Siamiri, callithrix sciureus, *Geoffroy Saint Hilaire, Annales du Museum,* xix. p. 113.—Sagoin siamiri, *Desmarest's Mammalogie,* p. 87.—Le Saïmiri, *Frederic Cuvier, Histoire Naturelle des Mammiferes.*

THIS beautiful and active little animal is scarcely more than ten inches in length, exclusive of the tail which is between thirteen and fourteen, and when seated, the height of the back was only about six. The upper parts of the body are of a greenish-yellow, which assumes a grayish tint on the thighs and arms; the feet, legs, and fore-arms are reddish chestnut, and the lower parts are nearly white. The muzzle is of a darker colour than the rest of the face, which, with the ears, is flesh-coloured. The tail is black at the tip. The nails, except those on the thumbs, have a somewhat claw-form.

A living specimen, which Frederic Cuvier describes, from the Royal Gardens, was very playful and good tempered. It never used its tail for a support, and

Stewart del.ᵗ   Lizars sc.

CALLITHRIX SCIUREUS.

(The Siamiri.)

when at rest it was either wound round its body or
limbs; when sleepy, it kept the tail in this position,
and the head between the forelegs, somewhat in the
manner in which the subject of the following plate
is represented. The *Siamiri* is a native of Brasil and
Cayenne, and is very often kept by the natives in
confinement. It is a common species, though we
seldom meet with it in collections. *

Another remarkable animal belonging to this group
is mentioned by Humboldt under the name of *Maca-
vacahow—Simia lugens.* It is extremely rare; one
specimen having only been seen by that naturalist,
who met with it in the forests bordering the Cassiquaire and Guaviaré. As far as he could learn, it
was one of those few species which live in pairs, and
that opinion is confirmed by the fear and dislike which
it exhibited when placed near even some of the most
diminutive species of the same genus.

It was extremely shy, and only when alone exhibited its activity; when persons were near, though
occupied with general business, it would remain for
hours in immovable attention to all that passed, refusing even food, though it had long fasted. But when
alone, the sight of a bird at once rouses it. It darts
upon it like a cat, swallows it in a second, and
in its whole manner at this time, resembles a small
carnivorous animal.

* There are good specimens in the Edinburgh Museum.

The colour of the body is a shining black, in some parts with a purplish lustre, and the texture of the hair is remarkably soft and shining. The face appears as a square mask of bluish-white, which is surrounded by a narrow margin of a purer tinge, and two stripes of the same colour run from the eyes to the temples; the throat is marked with a white band, and the hands are of the same colour on the outsides, somewhat resembling, and compared by the natives to a pair of white gloves; the tail is not much longer than the body, and not at all used as a prehensile instrument.

Eight species of this curious little group are described, which generally have the same habits, and show a beautiful gradation of both form and manners to some of the small carnivora. We are not sure that this is their proper situation, but prefer following the arrangement of Geoffroy and Desmarest. Any alterations which we could now make are only upon insufficient grounds.

The next form which succeeds in the system we have presently adopted, is one of as great singularity, and is yet represented by a single individual, discovered by Humboldt; it is,

PLATE 24

Stewart delt.

Lizars sc.

AOTES TRIVIRGATUS.
The Douroucouli.

THE DOUROUCOULI.

Aotes trivirgatus.—HUMBOLDT.

PLATE XXIV.

Le Douroucouli, Aotes trivirgatus, *Humboldt and Bonpland, Observations de Zoologie*, i. p. 306 ; *Geoffroy, Annales du Museum d'Histoire Naturelle*, xix. p. 115 ; *Desmarest's Mammalogie*, p. 88.

THIS curious animal, the only type yet discovered of the above-mentioned genus, was found during Humboldt and Bonpland's arduous journey upon the Oronooko ; and, as their descriptions alone exist, we have made use of the greater part of them in the following article, and also of their beautiful plate for the accompanying illustration. It may be characterised by the head, large and round ; muzzle short ; no apparent external ear ; the eyes very large ; the tail long, hairy, not prehensile ; habits nocturnal.

The *Douroucouli* of the Maravitain Indians is covered with a soft grayish-white fur, having a line of brown along the centre of the back, from the head to the tail ; the breast, belly, and inner part of the legs,

are yellowish-brown. The head is marked with three
dark stripes, very apparent in front, whence Hum-

boldt takes his name, and the missionaries of the
Oronooko that of " *Cara rayada.*" The general resemblance of the face is more like that of a cat than
of a quadrumanous animal; the eyes are very large,
and of a rich yellow; the mouth is surrounded with
strong white bristly hairs. The ears are not apparent
externally; the inside of the hands are white, and the
nails are flattened; the tail is much longer than the
body, of the same colour, except a black tip, bushy
and soft. The whole length of the body is nine
inches; that of the tail about fourteen. The skin
is so soft and pleasant to the touch, that it is often preserved for different purposes, and particularly for tobacco pouches.

The *Douroucouli* is the only monkey of the
Oronooko which sleeps during the day, whence it is
often called " *Mono dormillon.*" Humboldt kept one

alive for five months, and observed that it slept regularly from nine in the morning to seven at night; sometimes its sleep commenced even at daybreak, and light was always much disliked. When going to sleep, it selected the most shady place, behind some wood, or in the cleft of a tree, and, like the squirrels and weasels, had great facility in passing through very small holes or openings.

When disturbed during the day, it appears almost in a state of lethargy; it can scarcely raise its large white eyelids, and the eyes, which at night resemble those of an owl, are without lustre. In the ordinary sleeping position, it seats itself like a dog; the back is bent; the four hands brought together, and the head is almost concealed between them. It is at this time very stupid; may be touched without being bit, and its mouth may even be opened, and the teeth examined.

But if sluggish during the day, it is restless and all exertion at night. It now seeks its food; hunts small birds and insects, but in addition will eat almost every kind of vegetable. It was particularly fond of flies, which it took with great address, and was even tempted to hunt for them in a dull day. It drunk little, and would sometimes pass twenty or thirty days without tasting a liquid. Humboldt kept his specimen in the bedroom, notwithstanding the native opinion that they will tear out the eyes of persons asleep; it made extraordinary noises, and jumped against the walls, most probably in endeavours to escape. The *Douroucouli* is taken by the natives during the day when asleep, and half concealed in a hollow tree; and the male and female are sometimes taken in the same hole, as they resemble the last animal described, and live in pairs only.

This animal is very difficult to tame; the one above alluded to was carried sometimes in a canoe, sometimes on the back of a sumpter mule; and although caressed by every body, it constantly bit, was seldom playful, and seemed continually occupied with itself. Its nocturnal cry of *" Muh-muh,"* resembled the jaguar of America, and it has received from this the name of *Titi-tigre.* The voice is extremely powerful compared with its size, and consists in a sort of mewing *" e-i-aou,"* or a very disagreeable guttural cry of *" Quer-quer."* When irritated, the head is swelled, and in its hissing, and the position of its body, it resembles a cat attacked by a dog; it also strikes in the same manner with its paw, using it with great quickness.

This animal was seen by Humboldt in the thick forests bordering the Cassiquairé, those at the foot of Mount Duida, and near the Cataracts of the Maypures.

Such is the substance of Humboldt's description of this very curious animal, and which recedes even farther from the typical forms of the quadrumanous animals than the preceding, and presents a very strong alliance with many of the *Lemuridæ*, and some of the sloth-like animals. The anatomy and skeleton have not been sufficiently examined, and specimens will be desiderata with every naturalist who is interested in the History of the Mammaliæ.

The next form among the American monkeys is the *Pithecia* of Geoffroy, which are also nocturnal in their habits, and have received the appellation of " night apes," and also of " fox-tailed apes," from the bushy tail. They may be characterised by a facial angle of 60°. Head round; muzzle short; canine teeth longer than the others; the 'ail not prehensile, shorter than the body and bushy ; the nails short and bent ; gregarious; nocturnal. The first we shall describe is

THE COUXIO.

Pithecia satanas.—HUMBOLDT.

PLATE XXV.

Le Couxio, Pithecia satanas, *Humboldt and Bonpland, Observations de Zoologie*, p. 314; *Geoffroy Saint Hilaire, Annales
du Museum*, xix. p. 115.—Saki Couxio, *Desmarest's Mammalogie*, p. 89.

THE *Couxio* or *Couchio* was discovered by M. Sieber
in an expedition to Brasil, made at the expense of
Count Hofmannsegg, and described by that nobleman,
with some other animals, in a German periodical.
Humboldt has figured it in his Zoological Observations,
from one of the specimens now alluded to, and that
plate has served also for our illustration; it is represented eating the fruit of a species of palm.

The total length of the animal, including the tail,
is about two feet nine inches, and the colour is entirely of a dusky-black, paler beneath, where the hair is
very thin, and shews a purplish tinge, similar to that
of the face and hands.   The tail is very bushy; the
hair of it long and soft.   Little is known, except
that it is a native of the forests of Brasil.

Of another species we have more knowledge; and

PLATE 25

PITHECIA SATANAS

[The Couxio.]

Humboldt has recorded the history of the " *Capuchin de l'Oronoque*," the *P. chiropotes.* It is very si-milar to that just now described, except in colour, and the plate of the one might serve as an illustration of the other, if the tints were differently disposed. The colour is brownish-red, and the hair is long ; the beard is blackish-brown, arising below the ears, and covering a part of the breast. The eyes are large and sunk ; the tail is bushy, as in the last ; the claws are bent except on the thumbs.

Humboldt has given the following curious account of its manners : " Of all the monkeys of America, the *Capuchin* of the Oronooko has the greatest resemblance in its features to man. The eyes have a mingled ex-pression of melancholy and fierceness ; and as the chin is concealed by a long and thick beard, the facial angle appears much less than it really is. It is a strong, active, and fierce animal, and very difficult to tame ; when irritated, it raises itself upon the posterior ex-tremities, grinds the teeth, and leaps around the ag-gressor.

It very seldom drinks, and, when it does so, the action is performed, not like the other American mon-keys, which apply their lips to the liquid presented to them, but, taking the water up in the hollow of its hand, and inclining the head upon the shoulder, it carries it to the mouth. The operation is performed with great deliberation, and the spectator must remain concealed to witness it. The animal becomes furious when the beard is wetted ; and Humboldt is of opinion, that the method of drinking has been adopted, from the impossibility of the lips being applied to the water in the ordinary way, without wetting the beard.

The *Capuchin de l'Oronoque* is not gregarious, and the males are rarely found in company with the female. Their cry is hoarse and hollow, but is very seldom heard. They are found in the vast and desert forests of the High Oronooko, to the south-east of the Cataracts, but are rather uncommon ; and although said to be found in other parts of South America, were never elsewhere met with by the enterprising naturalists to whom we have now been indebted for so much information.

The next animal we shall mention, has been placed last in this genus by Desmarest, and seems to differ from the others considerably ; it is,

PLATE 2

Stewart del.

Lizars sc.

PITHECIA MELANOCEPHALA.
(The Cacajao.)

THE CACAJAO.

Pithecia melanocephala.—DESMAREST.

PLATE XXVI.

Le Cacajao, Simia melanocephala, *Humboldt and Bonpland, Observations de Zoologie,* i. pp. 317, 359 ; *Geoffroy Saint Hilaire, Annales du Museum,* xix. p. 117.—Saki cacajao, *Desmarest's Mammalogie,* p. 91.

THIS very curious and diminutive species was also discovered by Humboldt and Bonpland, and it is to their description and plate that we are indebted for all that is known regarding it. By the different native tribes it is called as above, and also *Caruiri, Mono feo, Chacuto,* or *Mono robon.* It is very rare, and a single individual was only met with by those travellers in an Indian hut at San Francisco Solano. It is scarcely more than a foot in length, and the tail is not much more than a sixth ; and its describer says " it is among the *Siamiris,* the *Sais,* and *Ouistitis,* what the *Magot* of Barbary is among the long-tailed *Macaques.*"

The head of the *Cacajao* is very round, naked, and of a dull black, in its physiognomy much resembling that of an old negro ; the hair on the head is directed forwards ; the eyes are large and sunk, and the eye-

brows are composed of strong bristles; the nose is flat,
and the separation of the nostrils wide; there is no
beard; the ears are bare, and very large; the body,
with the exception of the head and hands, is clothed
with yellowish-brown, straight, long and shining hair;
the breast, belly, and insides of the arms, are of a
clearer or lighter tint; the hands are black, the fingers
very long, the nails flattened; the tail is thick, of the
same colour with the body, and black at the end.

The *Cacajao* is a voracious animal, and eats all
kinds of fruit; it is, however, weak; very inactive; of
a mild temper, and easily frightened. It was very
timid in the company of some small Sapajous; and the
sight of a crocodile or serpent made it tremble violently.
When about to seize any object, it stretches out its
arms in the manner represented on the plate, and holds
it with difficulty from the great length and slenderness
of the fingers. It inhabits the forests of the Cassiquaire and Rio Negro, and lives in troops.

We have now reached the group of small animals,
which will conclude the first great division of the
quadrumanous animals, or what generally go under
the title of monkeys; by Geoffroy they are made to
form a family, which he denominates *Arctopitheci*,
and divides into two subgenera; the great distinction is their squirrel-like action, and carnive-
rous propensities, and in the nails being in the form
of sharp claws; the first genus has been denomi-

nated *Hapales* ;* from the soft nature of the fur it
may be thus characterised, and differs, as we shall
see in the sequel, very slightly from that which
follows. The facial angle about 50° ; the head round,
most prominent at the occiput ; claws, except on the
thumbs of the posterior extremities ; lower cutting .
teeth unequal and cylindrical. The first species we ⅰ
shall notice is,

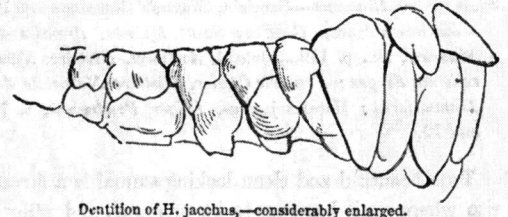

Dentition of H. jacchus,—considerably enlarged.

* Ἁπαλος —soft, delicate.

THE STRIATED MONKEY.

Hapales jacchus.—ILLIGER.

PLATE XXVII.

Simia jacchus, *Linnæus.*—Sanglain, *Edwards' Gleanings*, i. p. 1.*
—Jacchus vulgaris, *Geoffroy Saint Hilaire, Annales du
Museum*, xix. p. 119.—Ouistiti, *Audibert, Histoire Natu:
relle des Singes ; Frederic Cuvier, Histoire Naturelle des
Mammiferes ;* Hapales jacchus, *Illiger Prodromas,* p. 71
and 72.

THIS beautiful and clean-looking animal is a favourite whenever it happens to be procured, and after a
few hours restraint becomes playful and familiar. It
has been long known to naturalists, and the illustration taken from Audibert, which accompanies this
description, will give a tolerable idea of its general
appearance.

The length of the body is only about eight inches,
that of the tail above eleven ; the general shade of the
fur is a grayish-olive, darker, and almost approaching to black on the head and shoulders ; and the lower
part of the back and tail are barred or ringed with
circles, of a rich pale gray, which alternately shade
into each other ; the lower parts of the body and fore

Stewart.delt.   Lizars sc.

HAPALES JACCHUS.

[The Striated Monkey.]

parts of the extremities are brownish-gray. The
face is flesh-colour, and there is a white spot on the
forehead; but the most conspicuous marking in the
physiognomy of the animal, are two tufts of pale
or grayish white hair, of considerable length, which
spring round each ear. All the claws, except those
on the hinder parts, are hooked, and very thick. It
generally walks in a quadruped position, and uses
the fingers in one direction. In a wild state, the food
may be said to be almost every thing; fruits, roots,
and seeds, insects, and small or young birds. In confinement, it is even more varied. Edwards, who has
given us a very good figure of it in his Gleanings, in-
forms us that the specimen from which he made his
drawing, " fed upon biscuits, fruits, greens, insects,
snails, &c.; and that once when loosed, it suddenly
snatched a Chinese gold fish from a basin of water
killed, and devoured it; after this, Mrs Kennon, to
whom it belonged, gave it live eels, which frightened
him at first, by twisting round his neck, but he soon
mastered them and ate them."

They breed occasionally in confinement; Edwards
mentions a pair which had produced young in Portugal,
and Frederic Cuvier had two which bore young in
1819. The female produced three, but very soon
ate off the head of one of them; in the mean time the
others began to suck, and from the period of their
commencement, she was as affectionate as she was
before careless. The male seemed more affectionate

and careful of them than the mother, and assisted in the charge. The young generally keep upon the back or under the belly of the female, and Cuvier observed, that when the female was tired with carrying them, she would approach the male with a shrill cry, who immediately relieved her with his hands, placing the young upon his back, or under his belly, where they held themselves, and were carried about, till they became restless for milk, when they were given over to the mother, who, in her turn, would again endeavour to get rid of them. Cuvier is of opinion, however, that the general intelligence and penetration exhibited by this animal, is inferior to many of the smaller monkeys.

In general, the species of this genus have a part of the body and tail barred with a lighter shade. Some are again uniform in the colours. One is entirely of a silvery white, with a black tail, and all the exposed parts of the skin being a bright red flesh-colour, give a curious appearance to the animal. It has the common name of *Mico,* and will stand as *H. argentatus.*

Another species without the barring is the *H. melanurus,* or black-tailed *Ouistiti,* and which is considered by Khul to make the passage to the next genus *Midas,* or the *Tamarins.* This is our last genus in this division, and is characterised nearly as the preceding, but differs in the dentition ; the lower incisors are equal, and cut in a sloping direction ; the forehead

PLATE 28

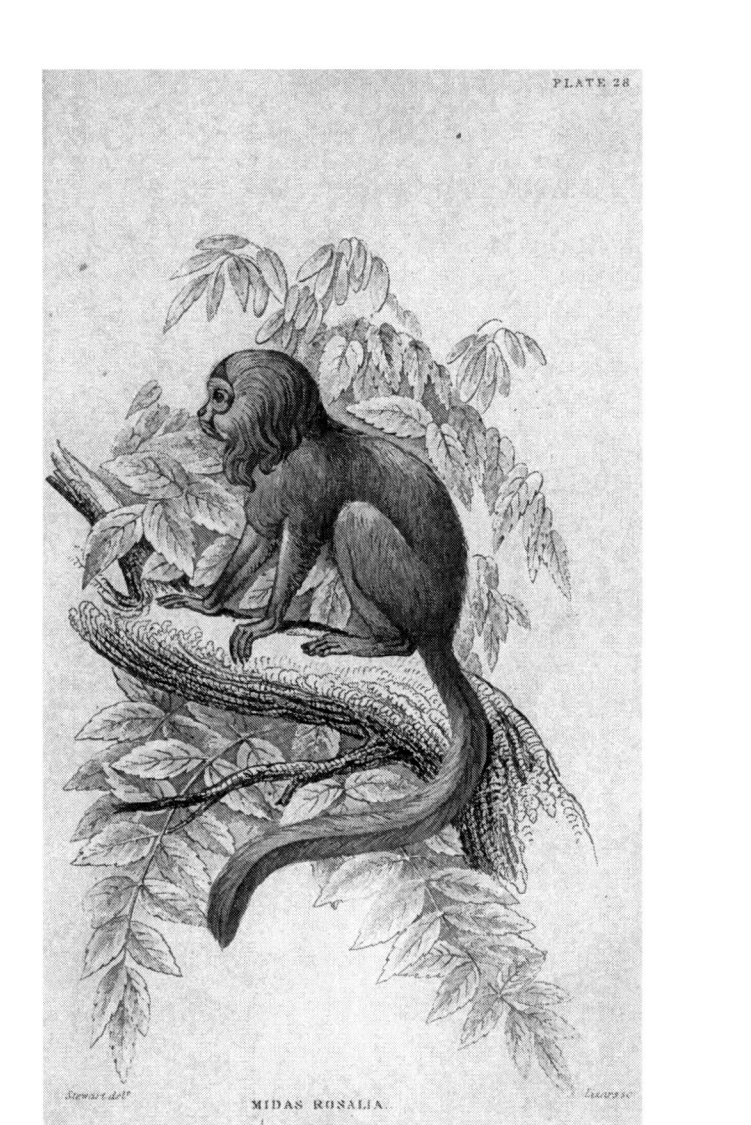

Stewart delt.

MIDAS ROSALIA.

[The Silky Tamarin]

Laurie sc.

appears more prominent by the projection of the or. bits.

One of the allying species is the *Midas ursulus* of Geoffroy, which is about the same size with the common *Ouistiti*, and has the back undulated with a black and brown colour, in a somewhat similar manner to that species; unlike it, however, this animal was very ill-natured, and showed his teeth upon the least motion near him, bit severely, or attempted it, when touched. One of the most pleasing in appearance is,

THE SILKY TAMARIN.

Midas rosalia.—GEOFFROY.

PLATE XXVIII.

Simia rosalia, *Linnæus.*—The silky monkey, *Shaw's Zoology.*— Midas rosalia, *Geoffroy Saint Hilaire, Annales du Museum,* xix. p. 121.—Le marikina, *Frederic Cuvier, Histoire Naturelle des Mammiferes.* — Ouistiti marikina, *Desmarest's Mammalogie,* p. 95.

THIS neat little animal is entirely of a clear golden yellow, palest on the back and thighs. The hair is very fine and silky, and so long upon the head and neck as to form a sort of ruffed mane, somewhat similar to the same part in the lion, and which has gained for it the name of the lion monkey. This species is often brought to Europe, and its beauty, and mild temper, and gentleness, render it a general favourite. They are, however, very tender, and the least damp causes them to droop, and if continued, kills them. Little is known of their native habits; but F. Cuvier thinks that they live a good deal in the manner of the squirrels, and that they remain almost constantly on the trees. He has never seen them attempt to stand upon the hinder extremities. The accompanying illustration is taken from the plate of Fred. Cuvier. The next animal we shall describe is perhaps the smallest monkey known, it is

PLATE 29

Stewart delt

Lizars sc

MIDAS LEONINA.

THE LEONINE TAMARIN.

Midas leonina.—GEOFFROY.

PLATE XXIX.

Simia leonina, Léoncito, *Humboldt, Observations de Zuorcgie*, p. 14, plate 5.—Tamarin leoncita, Midas leonina, *Geoffroy. Saint Hilaire, Annales du Museum*, xix. p. 121.—Ouistiti leoncita, *Desmarest's Mammalogie*, p. 95.

THIS curious little species was discovered by Humboldt and Bonpland during their travels in South America, and is described in the zoological researches of these naturalists.

The *Leoncito* is very rare; it inhabits the plains which border the eastern slope of the Cordilleras, the fertile rivers of Putumay and Caqueta. It never ascends to the more temperate districts, while the wandering bands of the *Marimonda* sometimes reach heights equal to those of the Caingow and Mount Perdu; it is about seven or eight inches in length. The *Leoncito* inhabits only the plains of Mocoa, and the tail nearly equals the body; it is extremely elegant; it is playful, but easily made angry. When en-

raged, or tormented, it bristles up the hair of the neck,
and increases its resemblance to a little lion. Its
activity was great, and when confined in a cage, it
was with difficulty the sketch was made. The cry
resembled the chirrup of some small bird. It was
found to breed occasionally when kept in the Indian
huts.

This is the account, and the only one, of this curious
monkey; few specimens exist in Europe, and I believe it has never been seen alive. With it we shall
conclude our review of this interesting section of the
quadrumanous animals, and refer to the Synopsis
which accompanies this volume, for the number and
characters of the species which have been authentically
described. It has been compiled from the works of
Geoffroy, Humboldt, Spix and Martius, and Desmarest; and whatever its imperfections may be, it will,
at least, contain the substance of the researches of
these illustrious zoologists. The remaining family of
the *Lemuridæ*, we shall endeavour to illustrate in a
future volume.

SYNOPSIS.

SYNOPSIS.

ORDER I. QUADRUMANA.[*]

Character of Order. Teeth of three kinds, incisor, canine, and molar.[†] Four extremities furnished with long and flexible hands, having opposable thumbs, chiefly formed for grasping. Clavicles complete. Bones of the limbs separate, and capable of pronation and supination. Pectoral mammæ, two or four. The orbital and temporal fossæ distinct. The stomach, simple. Food, fruits, roots, and insects. Habits, chiefly arboreal, living in forests or craggy precipices. Native countries, the warm parts of Africa, India, and America.[‡] Contains two great families, *Simiadæ* and *Lemuridæ*.

SYNOPSIS OF THE SIMIADÆ.

I. FAM. SIMIADÆ. Four incisive teeth in each jaw opposed. Nose, more or less prominent. Pectoral mammæ, generally two. (Two sub-families.)

    1. SUB. FAM. SIMIÆ CATARRHINI, *Monkeys of the Old World.* Number of teeth 32. Molar teeth, five on each side, crowned with blunt tubercles. Nostrils separated by a very narrow division. The tail never prehensile. With or without cheek-pouches and callosities. Inhabit the old world only.

---

[*] This is the second order of most zoologists.
[†] The Aye-aye, (*Cheiromys,* Cuvier,) alone wants the canine teeth.
[‡] Barbary ape, (*Inuus,* Cuvier,) alone reaches the southern border of Europe.

2. Sub. Fam. Simiæ platyrrhini, *Monkeys of the New World*. Number of teeth 36. Molar teeth on each side six. Nostrils separated by a broad division. The tail long; often prehensile. No cheek pouches or callosities. Inhabit the warm parts of Southern America.

I. SUB-FAMILY CATARRHINI.

ORANGS.

Genus I.—*Troglodites*, Geoffroy.

Muzzle short; facial angle 50°; ears large, and lying close to the head; arms comparatively short, reaching to the lower part of the thighs; tail, cheek-pouches, and callosities wanting.

᳂ Plate I.—1. T. niger, Black or African Orang.—*Geoff. Ann. du Mus.* xix. 87; *Desm. Mamm.* 49. Hair black, long and shaggy upon the back and shoulders; height of the adults, 5 to 6 feet; of the young seen in confinement in Europe, 2 to 3 feet. Inhabits the coasts of Angola and Congo.

Genus II.—*Pithecus*, Geoffroy.

Muzzle more lengthened than in the last; facial angle 65°; centre upper cutting teeth double in breadth to those at each side; canine teeth in the young not exceeding the others in length; in the adults twice as long, straight, and very strong; ears small; arms long; tail, cheek-pouches, and callosities wanting.

Plates II. and II*.—1. P. satyrus, Red or Asiatic Orang.— *Geoff. Ann. du Mus.* xix. p. 33; *Desm. Mamm.* p. 50; *Abel's Embass.* p. 319 and 365. Hair long and shaggy, shining reddish brown; adults very strong and powerful; height from 5 to 7 feet; young seen in confinement in Europe from 3 to 4 feet. Inhabits the interior

᳂ Refer to plates in this volume.

forests of Borneo and Eastern Asia. Most probably the Pongo.

Genus III.—*Hylobates*, Illiger.

Muzzle short; head round; facial angle 60°; canine teeth longer than the others; arms very long, reaching to the ground; tail and cheek-pouches wanting; with or without naked callosities.

Plate III.—1. H. hoolock, the Hoolock.—Simia hoolock, *Harl. Trans. of Am. Phil Soc.* Hair deep chocolate brown; face surrounded with a pale circle, most distinct on the forehead; no callosities. Inhabits Goalpara.

2. H. lar, Common Gibbon.—Simia lar, *Linn.* Pithecus lar, *Geoff. Ann. du Mus.* xix. p. 88; *Desm. Mamm.* p. 50. Hair black; the face surrounded with gray; small callosities on the buttocks. Inhabits Eastern India, particularly Coromandel, Malacca, and the Moluccas.

3. H. albimana,* White-handed Gibbon.—Simia albimana, *Vig.* and *Horsf. Zool. Jour.* No. xiii. p. 107. Hair black; the face surrounded with gray; the four hands whitish. Inhabits Sumatra.

4. H. variegatus, Little Gibbon.—Pithecus variegatus, *Geoff. Ann. du Mus.* xix. p. 88; *Desm. Mamm.* p. 51. Hair gray, varied with brown. Inhabits Malacca.

   Differs from the two preceding in the colour of the hair, and its less size; by many considered as a variety only, and not well established as a species.

5. H. leuciscus. The Wow-wow.—Pithecus leuciscus, *Geoff Ann. du Mus.* xix. p. 53; *Desm. Mamm.* p. 51. Hair ash gray; the face black, surrounded by a circle of light

* In the text of this volume we have followed Geoffroy Saint Hilaire in dedicating the entirely black species to Sir Stamford Raffles. It being, however, the old Linnean, *S. lar* must stand under that title, and the species with white hands has been named by Messrs Vigors and Horsefield as above.

gray; hands, feet, and ears, nearly black; callosities large.
Inhabits Malacca and the Sunda-Isles.

PLATE IV.—6. H. SYNDACTYLA. The Siamang.—Simia syndactyla.
Raff. Trans. Lin. Soc. xiii. p. 241; *Horsf. Java.* Hair black;
neck and upper part of the breast naked, and prominent from
the size of the laryngeal sacks; first and second finger of
lower extremities united to the end of the second phalanx;
callosities none. Inhabits Island of Sumatra.

PLATE V.—7. H. AGILIS.—The Active Gibbon.—*Fred. Cuv. Mammif.*
Hair clear brown, changing to a shining yellow on the back;
white band above the eyes; face bare, in the male blue, in the
female yellow; callosities small. Lives in troops, and displays very great agility. Inhabits Sumatra.

GUENONS.

GENUS IV.—*Presbytis*, ESCHSCHOLTZ.

Facial angle 60°; cheek-pouches none; callosities distinct; tail
long; arms reaching to the knees.

1. P. MITRULA, the Capped Monkey.—*Eschsch. in Kotzeb. Voy. of
Discov.* Hair curled, above bluish gray, beneath grayish white;
a black line from the upper part of the ears across the head;
length of the body about 1½ foot, tail long. Inhabits Sumatra.[*]

GENUS V.—*Colobus*, ILLIGER.

Muzzle short; nostrils approximated; tail longer than the body;
limbs slender; upper extremities without thumbs.

1. C. POLYCOMUS, Full-bottomed Monkey.—*Geoff. Ann. du Mus.*
xix. p. 92; *Desm. Mamm.* p. 53. Neck with a mane in the form
of a hood, covering the upper part of the back and shoulders,
variegated with black and fawn colour; body deep shining

[*] From Griffith's Animal Kingdom.

black; tail pure white. Inhabits the forests of Guinea and Sierra Leone.

2. C. FERRUGINOSUS, Bay Monkey.—*Desm. Mamm* ; p. 53. *Geoff. Ann. du Mus.* xix. p. 92. Bay Monkey, *Penn Quad.* Hair ferruginous; crown of the head, hands, and tail black. Inhabits Guinea.

3. C. TEMMINCKII, Temminck's Colobus.—*Khul. MSS.; Desm. Mamm.* p. 53. Upper parts, shoulders, and outer part of the thighs black; belly yellowish red; limbs clear red; face and tail reddish purple; length about 2 feet 8 or nine inches, including the tail. Native country unknown.

The only specimen known was purchased by M. Temminck, at the sale of Bullock's collection.

GENUS VI.—*Nasalis*, GEOFFROY.

Muzzle short; facial angle about 50°; the nose unproportionally lengthened; the nostrils at the extremity, on the under side; the body very thick; cheek-pouches and callosities; thumbs of anterior extremities slender; tail longer than the body.

PLATE VI.—1. N. LARVATUS, The Proboscis Monkey.—Hair reddish-brown; patched on the lower part of the back with lighter spots; face black. Inhabits Borneo.

2. N. RECURVUS, Turned-up Proboscis Monkey. Nasalis recurvus, *Vig. and Horsf. Zool. Journ.* xiii. p. 110. Hair reddish-brown, under parts paler; middle of the back and inside of the limbs gray; nose turned up. Inhabits Borneo.

Perhaps the young of *N. Larvatus.*

GENUS VII.—*Lasiopyga*, ILLIGER.

Facial angle from 50° to 60°; the muzzle only slightly elongated; face bare; hands longer than the fore-arm; thumbs on the anterior extremities short and slender; cheek-pouches; tail long; no callosities; the buttocks fringed with hair.

PLATE VII.—1. L. NEMEA, Cochin-China Monkey.—Pygathrix, *Geoff. Ann. du Mus.* xix. p. 90. Guenon Douc, *Desm. Mamm.* 54. Hair of brilliant colours; upper part of the head brown, with a frontal band of deep chestnut; hair of the cheeks very long, dirty white; fore-arms white, extending to the thumbs and fingers, which are black; tail white. Inhabits Cochin-China. (Madagascar, according to Harcourt.)

GENUS VIII.—*Semnopithecus*, CUVIER.

Head round; nose flat; facial angle 45°; limbs long; thumbs of anterior extremities very short; cheek-pouches and naked callosities; tail very long and thin; posterior grinder of the lower jaw with five points; form slender. India and Indian Archipelago.

PLATE VIII.—1. S. MELALOPHOS, the Simpai.—*Fred. Cuv. Mammif.* Simia melalophos, *Raff. Trans. Lin. Soc.* xiii. The face blue; forehead with a black band of long hairs, in the form of a tuft or crest; the hair of the upper parts clear red-brown; beneath, and in the inside of the limbs, tawny and whitish. Inhabits Island of Sumatra.

2. S. MAURUS, Negro Monkey.—Middle-size Black Monkey, *Edw. Glean.* S. maurus, *Horsf.* Hair soft and silky, intensely black; the breast, belly, inner surface of extremities and root of the tail, gray; in very old individuals, crown and upper parts tinged with gray. Inhabits Island of Java.

PLATE IX.—3. S. ENTELLUS, the Entellus Monkey. — Entelle, *Audeb.* Cercopithecus entellus, *Geoff. Ann. du Mus.*, xix. 95. Hair yellowish-white, paler beneath; face and hands black. Inhabits Bengal.

4. S. PYRRHUS, the Lutung.—*Horsf. Java.* Hair soft and silky; above, shining red; beneath, and inside the limbs,

fawn coloured. inhabits Java. (Allied to Cercopithecus auratus.)

5. S. PRUINOSUS.—*Desm. Mamm. Sup.* p. 533. Hair black, mixed with white, without a white spot at the origin of the tail, as in S. maurus: tail brown. Inhabits Sumatra. (Allied to S. maurus.)

6. S. COMATUS.—*Desm. Mamm. Supp.* p. 533. Hair above gray, beneath whitish ; tail tipped with white ; hair of the crown black, long, forming an aigrette behind, and concealing the ears. Inhabits Sumatra.

GENUS IX.—*Cercopithecus*, GEOFFROY.

The head round ; forehead receding ; facial angle 50° ; no superciliary ridges ; nose flat ; cheek-pouches and callosities ; tail longer than the body. Africa and India.

1. C. AURATUS, Golden Guenon.—*Geoff. Ann. du Mus.* xix. p. 93. *Desm. Mamm.* p. 56. Above, golden yellow ; beneath, paler ; black spot upon the knee ; hair of the breast and cheeks long. Inhabits India and Molucca.

2. C. TALAPOIN, the Talapoin Monkey.—*Penn. Quad.* 206. *Geoff. Ann. du Mus.* xix. p. 93. Hair above, olive ; beneath, yellowish-white ; feet black. Inhabits India, according to Buffon. (Described from Buffon. Supposed by F. Cuvier to be the young of Cercocebus cynosurus.)

3. C. LATIBARBUS, Purple-faced Bearded Monkey.—*Desm. Mamm.* p. 57. Guenon à face pourpre, *Buff.* Simia dentata, *Shaw.* *Adult*, hair woolly, black ; a large beard extending laterally ; tail tufted at the end. *Young*, hair entirely red. Native country unknown.

4. C. CEPHUS, Mustache Monkey.—Simia cephus, *Linn.* Guenon moustac, *Desm. Mamm.* p. 57. Hair greenish-brown, (according to Geoff. reddish-brown,) latter half of the tail white ; nose and lips blue. Inhabits Guinea, *Geoff.*

6. C. PILEATUS, Bonneted Monkey.—Simia pileata, *Shaw.* Guenon couronnée, *Desm. Mamm.* p. 57. Hair above brownish-yellow; beneath whitish; forehead adorned with long hairs erect in a tuft. Native country unknown. (Allied to Cercocebus sinicus.)

PLATE X.—C. MONA, Varied Monkey.—Simia mona, *Linn.* Guenon mone, *Desm. Mamm.* p. 58. Upper part of the head, bright yellowish-green; hair of the cheeks yellow; body deep chestnut, a white spot on each buttock. Native country uncertain, most probably Africa.

7. C. NICTITANS, White-nosed Monkey.—Guenon hocheur, *Desm. Mamm.* p. 58. Le hocheur, *Audeb.* Body black, sprinkled with greenish-gray; extremities black above; lower part of the chin white; nose more than usually long, white. Inhabits the coast of Guinea.

8. C. PETAURISTA, Vaulting Monkey.—Simia petaurista. *Linn.* Le blanc nez, and ascagne, *Audeb.* Hair above reddish, white below; outer part of the extremities greenish, inside gray; lower part of the nose white. Inhabits coast of Guinea.

PLATE XI.—9. C. RUBER, the Red Monkey.—Red monkey, *Penn.* Guenon patas, *Desm. Mamm.*, p. 59. Above reddish, gray beneath; hair of the cheeks long; a narrow band above the eyes black. Inhabits Senegal.

10. C. DIANA, Diana or Palatine Monkey.—Simia Diana, *Linn.* Exquina, *Margrave.* Guenon Diane, *Desm. Mamm.* p. 60. Hair of a deep chestnut on the back, dark gray on the flanks, with an oblique light line on the thighs; forehead adorned with a white crescent-shaped band; chin and throat white. Inhabits Congo and the Guinea coast.

11. C. ALBOCINEREUS, Grey guenon.—Guenon grisblanc, *Desm. Mamm. Supp.* p. 534. Hair gray above, lower parts whitish; a band of black crosses the forehead; extremities black; tail brown. Inhabits Island of Sumatra.

12. C. PYGERYTHRÆUS, Red-breasted Monkey.—*F. Cuv. Mammif.* Guenon Vervet., *Desm. Mamm. Supp.* p. 534. Above greenish-gray ; beneath white ; hair round the anus dull reddish ; tail tipped with black. Inhabits the Cape of Good Hope.

GENUS XII.—*Cercocebus*, GEOFFROY.

The muzzle lengthened ; the forehead receding : facial angle about 45° ; large cheek-pouches ; callosities large ; tail longer than the body. Africa and India.

PLATE XIII.—1. C. SABÆUS, the Callitrix or Green Monkey.—Simia sabea, *Linn.* Guenon callitriche, *F. Cuv. Mammif.* ; *Desm. Mamm.* p. 61. Singe vert, *Geoff. Ann. du Mus.* xix. p. 97. Above olive-green ; shaded beneath from yellowish-green to white ; face black, surrounded with long hair. Inhabits Cape de Verd islands, Senegal, the Mauritius.

2. C. CYNOSURUS, the Malbrouk. — Guenon Malbrouck, *F. Cuv. Mammif.* ; *Desm. Mamm.* p. 60. Cercopithecus cynosurus Malbrouc, *Geoff. Ann. du Mus.* xix. 96. Above olive-brown, shading to whitish on the under parts ; a white band above the eyes. Inhabits Bengal.

3. C. GRISEO VIRIDIS, the Grivet.—Le Grivet, *F. Cuv. Mammif.* Guenon grivet, *Desm Mamm.* p. 61. Grayish green, paler beneath ; tail gray for the whole length. Inhabits Africa. (Allied to the two preceding species.)

PLATE XII.—4. C. FULIGINOSUS, Mangabey or White Eyelid Monkey.—Le Mangabey, *F. Cuv. Mammif.* Guenon enfumée, *Geoff. Ann. du Mus.* xix. 97 ; *Desm. Mamm.* p. 62. Entirely of a gray sooty black, paler beneath ; the upper eyelids white and conspicuous. Inhabits Ethiopia.

5. C. ÆTHIOPS, White Collared Mangabey.—Cercocebe mangabey, *Geoff. Ann. du Mus.* xix. p. 97. Guenon mangabey, *Desm. Mamm.* p. 62. The crown chestnut-brown,

the upper parts purplish brown ; a white band surrounding
the back of the neck.   Inhabits Ethiopia.

6. C. ATYS, the Atys.—Simia atys, *Audeb.* Atys, *Geoff.
Ann. du Mus.* xix. p. 99. Guenon atys, *Desm. Mamm.*
p. 62. Entirely of a yellowish-white ; the naked parts of
the skin flesh-coloured.   (By Geoffroy it is said to be an
albino variety of some unknown species, and to inhabit
India.)

GENUS XIII.—*Macacus,* LACÉPEDE.

Facial angle about 40° or 45° ; muzzle elongated ; superciliary
ridges distinct ; canine teeth strong and large (longer than in the
preceding genus ;) the tail shorter than the third of the length of
the body, or more ; the form strong and compact.

PLATE XIV.—1. M. SILENUS, the Ouanderow.—Simia canina,
Penn. Macaque a crinière, *Cuv. Reg. An.* Papio silenus,
Geoff. Ann. du Mus. xix. p. 100. Macaque ouanderow,
Desm. Mamm. p. 63. Above black ; the hair of the back
of the neck long, and, with the beard, forming a thick ruff,
gray ; under parts gray ; tail ending with a tuft of hairs.
Inhabits the Island of Ceylon.

2. M. SINICUS, Chinese Monkey.—Simla sinica, *Linn.* Bonnet-chinois, *Audeb.* Cercocebe bonnet-chinois, *Geoff.
Ann. du Mus.* xix. p. 64. Macaque bonnet-chinois, *Desm.
Mamm.* p. 64. Chestnut-brown, paler beneath ; hair of
the crown long, and spreading out from the centre to the
sides.   Inhabits Bengal and Ceylon.

3. M. RADIATUS, the Toque.—Cercocebe toque, *Geoff. Ann.
du Mus.* xix. p. 98. Macaque toque, *Desm. Mamm* p. 64.
Above greenish-brown ; beneath gray ; hair of the crown
long, and spreading out from the centre to the sides.   Inhabits India.

Nos. 2 and 3 are closely allied to *Cercocebus,* and their station in
the System does not seem clearly established. They are interesting forms, and ought to be kept in view by the zoologist.

4. M. CYNOMOLOGUS, Hare-lipped Monkey.—Cercocebe aigrette and macaque, *Geoff. Ann. du Mus.* xix. p. 99.
Macaque, *Cuv. Hist. Nat. des Mammif.* Macaque
ordinaire, *Desm. Mamm.* p. 62. The male, above olive,
beneath grayish-white; feet black; canine teeth strong,
length, including tail, 3 feet 3 inches. The female less;
canine teeth weaker; hair of the crown directed towards
the centre, and forms a ridge or tuft to the occiput. Inhabits Guinea and interior of Africa, *Desm.* Java, *Geoff.*

VIGNETTE.—5. M. RHESUS, Rhesus Monkey or Pig-tailed Baboon.
—Magot rhesus, Inuus rhesus, *Geoff. Ann. du Mus.*
xix. p. 101; *F. Cuv. Hist. Nat. des Mammif.* Macaque maimon, *Desm. Mamm.* 66. " Upper part of
the body grayish-green ; tail short, and wrinkled at the
base ; buttocks golden-yellow; extremities gray."—*Desm.*
Inhabits Eastern India. and forests on the banks of the
Ganges.

6. M. NEMESTRINA, Brown Baboon.—Maimon, Inuus nemes-
trinus, *Geoff. Ann. du Mus.* xix. p. 101. Macaque brun,
Desm. Mamm. p. 66. " Above deep brown ; middle of
the head and a dorsal band black ; tail small and slender,
reaching to the middle of the thigh ; extremities and head
yellowish."—*Desm.* Inhabits Java and Sumatra.

The Synonymy of Nos. 5 and 6 have often been confounded. Their
situation is undetermined. Geoffroy places them with the
Barbary Ape, so does Mr Gray, rejecting entirely Cuvier's
genus *Inuus.* We have followed Desmarest, as most in ac-
cordance with our own opinion

There are, it is probable, other allied species which have not been
properly characterised. Desmarest mentions one above two
feet in length; the back above brownish-black; the shoulders
olive; the outer surface of the feet yellowish-gray ; under part
of the throat grayish-white belly yellowish; ears small,
white hairs behind each.

7. M. NIGER. Black Baboon —Cynocephale negre, *Desm.
Mamm. Supp.* p. 534. Black ape, Macacus niger, *Zool.*

Gardens, i. p. 169.   Entirely black; fur woolly; the hair on the head long, falling back, and forming a crest; tail a tubercle.   Inhabits islands of Indian Archipelago. *Desm.*

> Differs from the type in the elongation of the muzzle, and want of tail; by the former allied to the baboons, by the latter to the next genus *Inuus*.

Genus XIV.—*Inuus*, Cuvier.

Facia. angle about 40°; muzzle elongated; the hands lengthened; tail none, or a tubercle.

Plate XV.—1. I. sylvanus, Barbary Ape.—Simia inuus, *Linn.* Magot African, *Geoff. Ann. du Mus.* xix. p. 100.   Magot, *F. Cuv. Hist. Nat. des Mammif.*   Macaque magot, Macacus inuus, *Desm. Mamm* p. 67.   Above greenish-gray; paler underneath and in the inner sides of the limbs. Tail a short cutaneous tubercle.

BABOONS.

Genus. XV.—*Cynocephalus*, Brisson.

Facial angle from 30° to 35°; superciliary ridges prominent; muzzle long, truncated at the end where the nostrils are placed; tail as long as the body.

1. C. babuin, Little Baboon.—Petit papion, *Buff.*   Papion cynocephale, *Geoff. Ann. du Mus.* xix. p. 102.   Babuin, *F. Cuv. Hist. Nat. des Mammif.*   Cynocephale babuin, *Desm. Mamm.* p. 68.   Male, above yellowish-green, beneath paler; the face livid; cartilage of the nostrils not longer than the upper jaw.   Female unknown.   Inhabits Northern Africa.

2. C. papio, Guinea Baboon.—Papion, *Audeb.*   Papio sphinx, *Geoff. Ann. du Mus.* xix. p. 103.   Cynocephale papion, *Desm. Mamm.* p. 69.   Above brown, paler beneath; cheeks yellowish; face, ears, and hands, black; cartilage

of the nostrils longer than the jaws. In the young the muzzle is shorter. Inhabits the coast of Guinea.

PLATE XVI.—3. C. PORCARIUS, the Chacma.—Simia porcaria, *Linn.* Papio porcarius and comatus, Babuin porc and chevelu, *Geoff. Ann. du Mus.* xix. p. 102 and 103. Chacma, *F. Cuv. Hist. Nat. des Mammif.* Cynocephale chacma, *Desm. Mamm.* p. 69. Simia ursina, *Penn.* Greenish-black, palest on the fore part of the shoulders; hair long upon the neck, in the form of a mane; face violet black; upper eyelids white. Female without the mane. Inhabits Southern Africa, Cape of Good Hope.

4. C. HAMADRYAS, Dog-faced Baboon.—Simia hamadryas, *Linn.* Dog-faced ape, *Penn.* Tartarin, *Geoff. Ann. du Mus.* xix. p. 103; *F. Cuv. Hist. Nat. des Mammif.* Cynocephale tartarin, *Desm. Mamm.* p. 69. Blackish-gray tinged with brown; hair of the fore parts long, forming a shaggy mane; face flesh colour. Female and young with short muzzles, coloured blue. Inhabits Moco, borders of the Persian Gulf, Arabia.

GENUS XVI.—*Papio*, BRISSON.

Proportions much stronger than Cynocephali, and distinguished from them by the tail being very short, almost a tubercle, and perpendicular to the dorsal line. Dentition very powerful.

PLATE XVII.—1. P. MORMON, the Mandril.—Simia mormon, *Linn.* Variegated Baboon, *Penn.* Mandril, *Geoff. Ann. du Mus.* xix. p. 104; *F. Cuv. Hist. Nat. des Mammif.* Cynocephale mandril, *Desm. Mamm.* p. 70. Yellowish-olive, tinged with gray above, beneath white; beard yellow; muzzle furrowed; livid, but bright red and blue. In the young the furrows do not appear. Inhabits Africa, on the Gold and Guinea coast.

PLATE XVIII.—2. P. LEUCOPHÆUS, the Drill.—Simia leucophæa, *F. Cuv. Ann. du Mus.* ix.; *Hist. Nat. des Mammif.*

Cynocephale drill, *Desm. Mamm.* p. 71. Above greenish-brown tinged with gray, beneath white. Face of males, females, and young, uniform dull black. Under lip red. No furrows on the muzzle. Inhabits Africa.

> We have deviated from the text of the volume in dividing the *Cynocephali.* Though very closely allied, and by most writers united either under *Cynocephalus* or *Papio,* they are always divided into sections, and we generally prefer an entire separation to divisions of that kind.

> One or two baboons are mentioned by Pennant upon dubious authority, which it is not necessary to introduce here, as proper characters could not be given.

II. SUB-FAMILY PLATYRRHINI.

HOWLERS.

GENUS XVII.—*Mycetes,* ILLIGER.

Facial angle about 30°; canine teeth strong; tail long, prehensile, naked at the extremity on the under side; os hyoides ventricose, apparent on the outside; gregarious; howling during night; largest and fiercest of the South American group.

    1. M. SENICULUS, the Mono Colorado, or Red Howler.— Simia seniculus, *Linn.* Stentor seniculus, *Geoff. Ann. du Mus.* xix. p. 107. Mono colorado, *Humb. Obs. Zool.* p. 354. Alouate roux, *Desm. Mamm.* p. 77. Fur reddish-brown, brightest on the tail and extremities; under parts nearly hairless; face naked and black. Inhabits French Guiana, banks of the rivers Madeleine and Darien.

PLATE XIX.—2. M. URSINUS, the Araguato.—Stentor ursinus, *Geoff. Ann. du Mus.* xix. p. 108. Araguato de Caraccas, *Humb. Obs. Zool.* pp. 329 and 355. Alouate ourson, *Desm. Mamm.* p. 78. Entirely reddish-brown, and clothed with long hair on every part; bearded; face bluish-black. Inhabits Venezuela, New Barcelona, banks of the Oronooko.

> Differs from the preceding in the hair being very long, and in being clothed on the under parts.

3. M. STRAMINEUS, the Arabata.—Stentor stramineus, *Geoff.*
Ann. du Mus. xix. p. 108; *Humb. Obs. Zool.* p. 355.
Alouate arabate, *Desm. Mamm.* p. 78. Hair entirely
straw-yellow, darker, or of a brownish colour at the roots.
Inhabits Peru.

4. M. BELZEBUTH, the Guariba.—Simia Belzebuth, *Linn.*
Stentor fuscus, *Geoff. Ann. du Mus.* xix. p. 108.
Stentor guariba, *Humb. Obs. Zool.* p. 355. Alouate
guariba, *Desm. Mamm.* p. 78. Brownish-chestnut, passing into chestnut on the head and back; the tips of the
hair golden colour. Inhabits Brasil.

5. M. FLAVICAUDATUS, the Chora.—Stentor flavicaudatus,
Geoff. Ann. du Mus. xix. 108. Simia flavicauda, Chora,
Humb. Obs. Zool. p. 343 and 355. Alouate chora,
Desm. Mamm. p. 79. Brownish-black, darker on the
back; tail blackish-olive, adorned on the sides with two
yellow stripes. Inhabits the province of Jaen, banks of
the river Amazon.

6. M. NIGER, the Caraya.—Stentor niger, *Geoff. Ann. du
Mus.* xix. 108. Simia caraya, *Humb. Obs. Zool.*
p. 355. Alouate caraya, *Desm. Mamm.* p. 79. Rich
shining black; tail rather short; female and young with
the sides and under parts yellowish-brown. Inhabits Paraguay, Bahia.

7. M. RUFIMANUS, Red-Handed Howler. —Mycetes rufimanus, *Khul MSS.; Desm. Mamm.* p. 79. Black; wrists
and hands, and extreme half of the tail, reddish-brown;
lower parts nearly without hair. Native country unknown.
The description of this species is only known from the MSS. of
Khul, taken from a specimen purchased by M. Temmink at
the dispersion of Bullock's Museum.

SAPAJOUS.

GENUS XVIII.—*Ateles*, GEOFFROY.

Head round ; facial angle about 60° ; extremities proportionally very long and slender ; the anterior hands with four fingers, or the thumb supplied by a rudiment only ; tail very long ; powerfully prehensile, having a part without hair, covered with a very delicate and sensible skin on the under side ; os hyoides large, but not apparent from the outside ; habits and movements slow and indolent.

1. A. HYPOXANTHUS, the Miriki.—Atèle hypoxanthe, *Desm. Mamm.* p. 72. Of a yellowish-gray ; vent and base of the tail often reddish-yellow ; face flesh-colour ; thumb a short rudiment, furnished with a nail. Inhabits Brasil between the 13° and 23° of S. latitude.

2 A. SUBPENTADACTYLUS, the Chameck.—Atèle chameck, *Geoff. Ann. du Mus.* xix. 105 ; vii. 267 ; *Desm. Mamm.* p. 73. Chameck, *Humb. Obs. Zool.* p. 353. Entirely black ; thumb a rudiment, without a nail. Inhabits French Guiana and Peru.

PLATE XX.—3. A. PANISCUS, the Coaita.—Simia paniscus, *Linn.* Atèle paniscus, *Geoff. Ann. du Mus.* xix. p. 105 ; vii. 269. Atèle coaita, *Desm. Mamm.* p. 73. Coaita, *Humb. Obs. Zool.* i. p. 352 ; *Fred. Cuv. Hist. Nat. des Mammif.* Entirely black ; thumb wanting on the anterior extremities. Inhabits Guiana, Brasil.

Distinguished from the last by the less size, and want of the thumb on the anterior hands.

4. A. BELZEBUTH, the Marimonda.—*Geoff. Ann. du Mus.* xix. p. 106 ; vii. p. 271. Atèle belzébuth, *Desm. Mamm.* p. 74. Marimonda de l'Oronoque, *Humb. Obs. Zool.* i. pp. 327, 353. Dusky black, under parts yellowish-white in the males ; white in the female and young. Inhabits banks of Oronooko.

5. A. MARGINATUS, the Chuva.—*Geoff. Ann. du Mus.* xiii.

p. 90 ; xix. p. 106. Atèle chuva, *Desm. Mamm.* p. 75.
Chuva, *Humb. Obs. Zool.* p. 354. Black: face surrounded
with white or yellowish ; breast and insides of the limbs
grayish-white. Inhabits province of Jaen, banks of the
rivers Santiago and Amazons.

6. A. ARACHNOIDES, Spider Monkey.—*Geoff. Ann. du
Mus.* xiii. p. 90 ; xix. p. 109. Simia arachnoides, *Humb.
Obs. Zool.* p. 354. Atèle arachnoide, *Desm. Mamm.*
p. 75. Grayish-yellow ; fur very soft ; eyebrows black.
Inhabits Brasil.

7. A. MELANOCHIR, Black-Handed Coaita.—Atèle melono-
chiere, *Desm. Mamm.* p. 76. Gray ; upper part of the
head, hands, and an oblique spot upon the knees, brownish-
black. Native country unknown.

Described by Desmarest, from a specimen in the Collection at
Paris.

GENUS XIX.—*Lagothrix*, HUMBOLDT.

Head round ; facial angle about 50° ; hands with five fingers ;
tail strongly prehensile, naked and callous on the under side of the
extremity ; os hyoides slightly apparent on the outside.

1. L. HUMBOLDTII, the Capparo.—Simia lagotricha, le capparo
du Rio Guaviare, *Humb. Obs. Zool.* i. pp. 322, 354.
Lagothrix Humboldtii, *Geoff. Ann. du Mus.* xix. p. 107.
Lagotriche capparo, *Desm. Mamm.* p. 76. Grayish-
black ; hair long and soft. Inhabits banks of the
Guaviare.

2. L. CANUS, Gray Lagothrix.—*Geoff. Ann. du Mus.* xix.
p. 107. Lagotriche grison, *Desm. Mamm.* p. 77. Grayish-
olive ; head, hands, and tail, reddish-gray ; the hair very
short. Inhabits Brasil.

GENUS XX.—*Cebus*, XERLEBEN.

The head round ; muzzle short ; facial angle about 60° ; os
hyoides small ; hands, with a lengthened well-formed thumb ; tail

long, prehensile, entirely covered with hair; gregarious; habits lively, active.

1. C. APELLA, the Weeper Sapajou.—Simia apella, *Linn.* Sajou, *Audeb.* Sajou brun, *Geoff. Ann. du Mus.* xix. p. 109. Sapajou sajou, *Desm. Mamm.* p. 81. Deep brown above, of a clearer and lighter shade beneath; crown, feet, and tail, blackish-brown; face generally surrounded with a lighter shade. Inhabits Guiana. (Not found in Brasil,—(*P. Maximilien.*)

This species is subject to considerable variety in the shade of the colours.

2. C. ROBUSTUS. Prince Maximilien's Sapajou.—Sapajou robuste, *Desm. Mamm.* p. 80. Brown; upper part of the head, neck, and a circle round the face, black; arms clear yellowish; fore part of the neck and belly in the male chestnut-red; in the young and females, yellowish or fawn colour. Inhabits Brasil. (Does not pass the river Doce to the South.—*P. Maximilien.*)

3. C. GRISEUS. Gray Sapajou.—Sapajou gris, *Desm. Mamm.* p. 81. Sajou, *F. Cuvier, Hist. Nat. des Mammif.* Above yellowish-brown, mingled with gray; below of a clear fawn colour; crown black; face surrounded with black; sometimes white upon the neck and breast. Inhabits Guiana.

A variety is described by Desmarest with the upper parts yellowish-brown, paler beneath; crown black; sides of the head, anterior part of forearms, neck. and breast, white; face flesh-colour. This is described from a single specimen, not adult, and most probably distinct, the markings being so different.

4. C. BARBATUS, Bearded Sapajou.—Cebus albus, *Geoff. Ann. du Mus.* xix. p. 112. Sapajou barbu, *Desm. Mamm.* p. 82. Grayish-red; under parts reddish; beard lengthened upon the cheeks, dark chestnut; hair long and crisp. Inhabits Guiana.

Varies according to age to gray and white. We have followed Desmarest in considering Geoffroy's Cebus albus as one of the above varieties.

5. C. TREPIDUS, Tufted-tailed Sapajou.—Simia trepida, *Linn.* Cebus frontatus, *Kuhl.* Cebus trepidus, Sajou tremblens, *Geoff. Ann du Mus.* xix. p. 110. Sapajou coeffé, *Desm. Mamm.* p. 82. Nearly of a uniform black shade ; dusky on the head and extremities ; scattered white hairs around the mouth and upon the anterior hands ; hair of the forehead raised. Inhabits Dutch Guiana.—*Geoff.*

6. CEBUS NIGER, Negro sapagou.—Cebus niger, Sajou nègre, *Geoff. Ann du Mus.* xix. p. 111. Sapajou nègre, *Desm. Mamm.* p. 83. Deep brown ; face, hands, and tail black ; forehead and cheeks mixed with yellowish hairs. Native country unknown.

7. CEBUS VARIEGATUS, the Varied Sapajou.—Cebus variegatus, *Geoff. Ann. du Mus.* xix. p. 111. Simia variegatua, *Humb. Obs. Zool.* i. p. 356. Sapajou varié, *Desm. Mamm.* p. 83. Body blackish, sprinkled with golden-yellow ; hair very soft, long, and of three colours—brown at the root, red, and black. Inhabits Brasil.—*Geoff.*

The hair of this monkey resembles that of the true Guenons in the variation of colour.

8. CEBUS FLAVUS, Yellow Sapajou.—Simia flava, *Schrœber.* Sajou flave, Cebus flavus, *Geoff. Ann. du Mus.* xix. p. 112. Sapajou fauve, Cebus fulvus, *Desm. Mamm.* p. 83. General colour dull yellowish-brown, tinged with gray and brown on the head ; the hair silky and straight ; young with the head, tail, and limbs, chestnut-red. Inhabits Brasil.

9. CEBUS ALBIFRONS, the Ouavapavi.—Ouavapavi, Simia albifrons, *Humb. Obs. Zool.* i. p. 323, 356. Cebus albifrons, *Geoff. Ann. du Mus.* xix. p. 111. Sapajou ouavapavi, *Desm. Mamm.* p. 83. Gray ; lighter on the under parts ; crown black ; forehead and orbits white brownish-yellow. Inhabits banks of Oronooko, near Cataracts.

10. Cebus lunatus, Lunulated Sapajou.—Cebus ?:<atus, *Kuhl.* Sapajou lunule, *Desm. Mamm.* p. 84. Black; a spot in the form of a crescent on each cheek, from the eyebrow to the mouth. Native country unknown.

Described by Kuhl from a specimen in the Academy of Heidelberg.

11. Cebus xanthosternos, Yellow-breasted Sapajou.—Sapajou a poitrine jaune, *Desm. Mamm.* p. 84. Chestnut; face and forehead yellowish-white; breast and lower part of the neck clear yellowish-red. Inhabits Brasil, between the 15° S. and the river Belmont.—*Desm.*

Plate XXI.—12. C. fatuellus, Horned Sapajou. — Simia fatuellus, *Linn.* Sajou cornu, *Audeb. Hist. Nat. des Singes; Geoff. Ann. du Mus.* xix. p. 109; *F. Cuv. Hist. Nat. des Mammif.* Sapajou cornu, *Desm. Mamm.* p. 84. Deep blackish-brown, face surrounded with whitish; hair of the front rising in two lengthened tufts above the eyebrows. Inhabits Guiana.

Is closely allied to *C. robustus*, and united with it by Humboldt. Subject to considerable variety.

13. C. cirrifer, Crowned Sapajou.—Sajou à toupet, *Geoff. Ann. du Mus.* xix. p. 110. Simia cirrifera, *Humb. Obs. Zool.* i. p. 356. Sapajou à toupet, *Desm. Mamm.* p. 84. Brownish-chestnut; crown, extremities, and tail, of a deeper tint, approaching black; a tuft of hairs on the highest part of the forehead. Inhabits Brasil.

14. C. capuchinus, Capuchin sapajou.—Simia capuchina, *Linn.; Humb. Obs. Zool.* i. p. 354. Sajou saï, *Geoff. Ann. du Mus.* xix. p. 111. Sapajou saï, *Desm. Mamm.* p. 85. Varying from grayish-brown to olive; crown and extremities black; front, cheeks, and shoulders whitish Inhabits Guiana.

Varies considerably. Hands sometimes of the same colour with the body.

15 C. hypoleucus, White-throated Sapajou.—Saï à gorge

blanche, *Audeb.* Simia hypoleuca, Cariblanco, *Humb.*
Obs. Zool. p. 356. Sapajou gorge blanche, *Desm. Mamm.*
p. 85. Black ; front, sides of the head, throat, and shoulders,
white. Inhabits Guiana.

PLATE XXII.—16. C. MONACHUS, Large-headed Sapajou.—Le
saï a grosse tête, Cebus monachus, *F. Cuv. Hist. Nat. des
Mammif.* A mixture of black and brown, irregularly
disposed, covers the back and sides ; breast, belly, sides of
the cheeks, and anterior part of arm, whitish-orange ; fore
arms, thighs, and tail, black ; a short black beard ; head
large. Native country unknown.

Sometimes varied on the upper parts with white. Described by
F. Cuvier from a living specimen.

GENUS XXI.—*Callithrix,* CUVIER.

The head round ; muzzle short ; facial angle about 60°. Separation of the nostrils narrower than the range of the upper cutting
teeth ; tail long, entirely hairy, not prehensile ; nails straight,
raised, and somewhat claw-like. Animals of small size.

PLATE XXIII.—1. C. SCIUREUS, Squirrel callithrix, or Siamiri.
Simia sciurea, *Linn. ;* Siamiri, *Audeb. ; F. Cuv. Hist.
Nat. ; Desm. Mamm.* Titi de l'Oronoque, *Humb. Obs.
Zool.* i. 322 and 257. Sagoin siamiri, *Desm. Mamm.*
p. 86. Grayish-brown, with a black muzzle ; extremities
bright reddish ; length of the body seven inches ; tail between thirteen and fourteen. Inhabits Brasil, Cayenne.

Varies in being entirely of one shade of brown, and with the
back bright reddish and black.

2. C. PERSONATUS, Masked callithrix.—Callithrix à masque,
Geoff. Ann. du Mus. xix. p. 113. Simia personata,
Humb. Obs. Zool. i. p. 357. Sagoin a masque, *Desm.
Mamm.* p. 86. Grayish-yellow ; head and the four hands
black ; tail reddish. Inhabits Brasil between the 18° and
21° of south latitude.

3 C. LUGENS, Mourning callithrix.—Veuve, *Geoff. Ann. du
Mus.* xix. p. 113. La viduita de l'Oronoque, *Humb.
Obs. Zool.* i. p. 319—357. Sagoin veuve, *Desm. Mamm.*
p. 87.   Black; throat and anterior hands white; tail
scarcely longer than the body.   Inhabits banks of the rivers
Guaviare and Cassiquaire.   Not gregarious.

4. C. AMICTUS, Ruffed callithrix.—Callithrix à fraise, *Geoff.
Ann. du Mus.* xix. 114.   Simia amicta, *Humb. Obs.
Zool.* p. 357.   Sajou a fraise, *Desm. Mamm.* p. 87.
Brownish-black; throat white; anterior hands dusky yel-
low; tail a fourth longer than the body.   Inhabits Brasil.

5. C. TORQUATUS, Collared callithrix.—Callithrix à collur,
Hoffmann, Geoff. Ann. du Mus. xix. p. 114. Simia tor-
quata, *Humb. Obs. Zool.* i. p. 357. Sagoin a collier,
Desm. Mamm. p. 87. Chestnut-brown; yellowish beneath;
throat white, in the form of a collar.   Inhabits Brasil.
Known only by the description of Count Hoffmannsegg.

6. C. MOLOCH, the Moloch.—Cebus moloch, *Hoffmann.
Moloch, Geoff. Ann. du Mus.* xix. p. 114. Simia mo-
loch, *Humb. Obs. Zool.* i. p. 158. Sajou moloch, *Desm.
Mamm.* p. 37.   Gray; temples, cheek, and belly, bright
reddish ; hands, and end of the tail, nearly white. Inhabits
Peru.

7. C. MELANOCHIR, Black-Handed Callithrix.—Prince Maximilien, Sagoin aux mains noires, *Kuhl ; Desm. Mamm.*
Gray lower part of the back ; end of the tail reddish ; anterior hands dull black ; inhabits Brasil.
Known only by the description of Kuhl.

8. C. INFULATUS, Mitred Callithrix.—Saguin Mitré, *Kuhl;
Desm. Mamm.* p. 89.   Gray above; reddish-yellow beneath ; a large white spot, surrounded with black, beneath
the eyes; end of the tail black ; inhabits Brasil.
Known by the description of Kuhl and Lichtenstein.

Genus XXII.—*Aotes*, Humboldt.

Head round, proportionally large; muzzle short; facial angle about 60°; separation of the nostrils narrow; ears small; tail longer than the body; not prehensile; nails flat; eyes and habits nocturnal; live in pairs.

Plate XXIV.—1. Aotes trivirgatus, The Douroucouli.—Simia trivirgata, Douroucouli, *Humb. Obs. Zool.* i. p. 307 and 358.   Aote Douroucouli, *Desm. Mamm.* p. 88; *Illig. Prod.* p. 71.   Gray; the belly reddish-yellow; forehead marked with three dark longitudinal stripes. Inhabits thick forests on the banks of the Cassiquaire.

Genus XXIII.—*Pithecia*, Desmarest.

Head round; muzzle short; facial angle 60°; canine teeth very strong; ears of middle size; tail shorter than the body, and covered with very long hairs; nails claws-like, short, and bent; habits nocturnal.

Plate XXV.—1. P. satanus, The Cuxio.—Couxio, *Geoff. Ann. du Mus.* xix. p. 115; *Humb. Obs. Zool.* i. p. 314. pl. 27.   Saki Couxio, *Desm. Mamm.* p. 89.   Hair brownish-black; furnished with a thick beard; breast and belly nearly hairless; female brownish-red.   Inhabits the banks of the Oronooko.

2. P. chiropotes, Hard-drinking Saki.—Capuchin, *Geoff. Ann. du Mus.* xix. p. 116; *Humb. Obs. Zool.* i. p. 358.   Saki capuchin, *Desm. Mamm.* p. 89.   Reddish-brown: hair of the head thick, divided in the middle in two tufts; beard long and thick; tail blackish-brown. Inhabits the forests of the High Oronooko, to the south and east of the Cataracts.

3. P. rufiventer, Red-bellied Saki.—Saki à ventre noux. *Geoff. Ann. du Mus.* xix. p. 116; *Desm. Mamm.* p. 90. Simia rufiventer, *Humb. Obs. Zool.* i. p. 358.   Brown, tinted with reddish; belly reddish-brown; hair on the

crown separating and falling down in front; beardless
Inhabits French Guiana.

4. P. MONACHUS, the Monk.—Moine, *Geoff. Ann. du Mus.*
xix. p. 116. Simia monachus, *Humb. Obs. Zool.* i. p.
359. Saki moine, *Desm. Mamm.* p. 91. Varied with
spots of brown and dusky-yellow; hair of the head elongated; tail as long as the body. Inhabits Brasil.

5. P. MIRIQUOUINA, the Miriquouina.—Miriquouina Azara,
Hist. of Parag.; Geoff. Ann. du Mus. xix. p. 117.
Simia Azaræ, *Humb. Obs. Zool.* i. 359. Saki miriquouina,
Desm. Mamm. p. 90. Gray; underneath reddish; hairs
on the back ringed with black and white; a white spot
above each eye. Inhabits the province of Chaco, and the
south bank of the river Paraguay.

6. P. LEUCOCEPHALA, the Yarke.—Yarke, *Buff.* Simia
leucocephala, *Humb. Obs. Zool.* i. p. 359. Pithecia
leucocephala, *Geoff. Ann. du Mus.* xix. p. 117. Saki
yarquè, *Desm. Mamm.* p. 91. Black, with the head
whitish; tail nearly the length of the body. Inhabits
Guiana.

PLATE XXVI.—7. P. MELANOCEPHALA, the Cacajao.—Simia
melanocephala, *Humb. Obs. Zool.* i. p. 359. Cacajao,
Humb.; Geoff. Ann. du Mus. xix. 117. Saki cacajao
Desm. Mamm. p. 91. Hair yellowish-brown; head and
tip of the tail black; tail, a sixth of the length of the
body. Inhabits the forests bordering the Cassiquaire and
Negro.

8. P. RUFIBARBA, Red-bearded saki.—Saki à moustach-
rouses, *Desm. Mamm.* p. 90. Upper part of the body
brownish-black, under part pale-red; eyebrows reddish;
tail slender toward the tip. Inhabits Surinam.
Described by Kuhl, from Temmink's Collection.

9 P. OCHROCEPHALA, Yellow-headed saki.—Saki à tête
jaune, *Desm. Mamm.* p. 90. Hair above of a clear-

chestnut, beneath yellowish-gray ; four hands brownish-black ; face surrounded with a circle of ochreous-yellow. Inhabits Cayenne.

Described by Kuhl, from Temmink's Collection.

GENUS XXIV.—*Hapales*, ILLIGER.

Muzzle short ; facial angle 60°.   The upper lateral incisors insulated ; the under lateral incisors longest ; inferior canine teeth very small ; nails, except those of the hinder thumbs, in the form of claws ; tail longer than the body, and squirrel-like.

PLATE XXVII.—1. H. VULGARIS, Ouistiti, or the Striated Monkey.—Ouistiti vulgare, Jacchus vulgaris, *Geoff. Ann. du Mus.* xix. 119; *Desm. Mamm.* 92.   Simia jacchus, *Humb. Obs. Zool.* i. p. 365.   Deep gray ; lower part of the back and tail banded with brown ; head of a chestnut-red ; forehead with a white spot ; the hairs from the cheeks and behind the ears nearly white, and very long.   Inhabits Guiana and Brasil.

Desmarest mentions a variety with the fur red, tinged with gray.

2. H. PENICILLATUS, The Tufted Ouistiti.—Pinceau, *Geoff. Ann. du Mus.* xix. 119.   Ouistiti pinceau, Jacchus penicillatus, *Desm. Mamm.* p. 94.   Simia penicillata, *Humb. Obs. Zool.* i. p. 365.   Gray ; tail and lower part of the back banded with brown ; forehead with a white spot ; hairs of the cheeks and behind the ears long and black.   Inhabits Brasil.

3. H. LEUCOCEPHALUS, White-headed Ouistiti.—Ouistiti à tête blanche, Jacchus leucocephalus, *Geoff. Ann. du Mus.* xix. 119; *Desm. Mamm.* 94.   Simia Geoffroyi, *Humb. Obs. Zool.* i. 365.   Hair red ; head and breast white ; neck black ; tail tinged with brown and gray ; hair behind the ears black and long.   Inhabits Brasil.

4. H. AURITUS, Eared Ouistiti.—Ouistiti oreillard, Jacchus auritus, *Geoff. Ann. du Mus.* xix. 119; *Desm. Mamm.*

p. 95. Simia aurita, *Humb. Obs. Zool.* i. 356. Hair black, mixed with brown ; tail tinged with black and gray ; a white spot on the forehead ; long white hair hides the interior of the ears ; *young* brown ; the *adult* markings obscure. Inhabits Brasil.

Nos. 2 and 4 are much allied to *H. vulgaris*.

5. H. HUMERALIFER, White-shouldered Ouistiti.——Ouistiti camail, Jacchus humeralifer, *Geoff. Ann. du Mus.* xix. p. 120 ; *Desm. Mamm.* p. 95. Simia humeralifera, *Humb. Obs. Zool.* i. 365. Hair brownish-chestnut ; tail slightly tinged with gray ; shoulders, breast and arms, white. Inhabits Brasil.

6. H. ARGENTATUS, The Mico.——Simia argentata, *Linn.* ; *Humb.*——Mico. *Audeb.* Ouistiti mico, Jacchus argentatus, *Geoff. Ann. du Mus.* xix. p. 120 ; *Desm. Mamm.* p. 94. Hair shining, entirely white ; the tail black ; face and hands deep flesh-colour. Inhabits Para.

According to Kuhl the tail is sometimes white.

7. H. ALBIFRONS, White-fronted Ouistiti.——Ouistiti à front blanc, Jacchus albifrons, *Desm. Mamm. Supp.* p. 534. Hair black ; white at the roots ; face black ; forehead, sides of the neck and throat, clothed with short white hair ; hair of the occiput and behind the ears long and black ; tail brown, slightly varied with white. Native district unknown.

8. H. MELANURUS, Black-tailed Ouistiti.——Ouistiti melanure, Jacchus melanurus, *Geoff. Ann. du Mus.* xix. p. 120. ; *Desm. Mamm.* p. 94. Simia melanura, *Humb. Obs. Zool.* i. p. 365. Hair brown above ; beneath yellowish ; tail of a uniform black. Inhabits Brasil, *Humboldt.*

Probably forms the passage to the next genus, *Midas*.

GENUS XXV.——*Midas*, GEOFFROY.

Muzzle short ; facial angle 60° : forehead appearing prominent, by the great angle of the upper edge of the orbits; upper incisors contiguous, under incisors equal in size; two inferior canine teeth nearly equal in size to the upper; nails, except on the hinder thumbs, formed like claws; tail as in *Hapales.*

1. M. RUFIMANUS, Red-Handed Tamarin.—Simia midas, *Linn. Humb.* Tamarin, *Audeb.* Tamarin a mains rousses, *Geoff. Ann. du Mus.* xix, p. 121. Ouistiti tamarin, *Desm. Mamm.* p. 94. Hair black; lower part of the back varied with gray; four hands reddish. Guiana. (Not found in Brasil, *Desm.*)

2. M. URSULUS, The Negro Tamarin.—Tamarin negre, *Audeb; Geoff. Ann. du Mus.* xix. p. 121. Ouistiti negre, *Desm. Mamm.* p. 94. Hair black; back waved with bright reddish; hands black. Inhabits Para.
Allied to the preceding.

3. M. LABIATUS, White-lipped Tamarin.—Tamarin labié, *Geoff. Ann. du Mus.* xix. p. 121. Ouistiti labié, *Desm. Mamm.* p. 95. Hair blackish, reddish beneath; head black; nose and lips white. Inhabits Brasil.

4. M. CHRYSOMELAS, Yellow-fronted Tamarin. Ouistiti à front jaune, *Desm. Mamm.* p. 95. Hair black; forehead and upper side of the tail golden-yellow; forehead, knees, breast, and sides of the head, of a chestnut-red. Inhabits Brasil and Para.

PLATE XXVIII.—5. M. ROSALIA, The Marikina, or Silky Tamarin. Simia rosalia, *Linn. Humb.* Marikina, *Buff. Audeb. Geoff.* Ouistiti marikina, *Desm. Mamm.* p. 95. Hair of a golden yellow, varying from a yellower to a rodder tinge; a main upon the neck. Inhabits Guiana, and the southern regions of Brasil, from Rio Janeiro to Cape Frio.
Desmarest mentions a variety from Guiana, varied with red and black—from Brasil, bright shining red.

PLATE XXIX.—6. M. LEONINUS, Leonine Tamarin. Simia leonina, *Humb. Obs. Zool.* i. 361. Leoncito, *Geoff.*

Ann. du Mus. xix. i. 121. Ouistiti leoncito, *Desm. Mamm.* p. 95. Hair brownish; neck with a mane of the same colour; face black; mouth white; tail black above, white beneath. Inhabits the plains which border the eastern part of the Cordilleras.

7. M. ŒDIPUS, The Pinche.—Simia œdipus, *Linn.* Pinche, *Audeb.* Titi de Carthagene, *Humb. Obs. Zool.* i. 337. Pinche, *Geoff. Ann. du Mus.* xix. p. 122. Ouistiti pinche, *Desm. Mamm.* p. 96. Hair brownish yellow above, white beneath; a long beard, silky and white; tail red, extreme half black. Inhabits Carthagena, rare in Gaiana

APPENDIX.

A FEW

OBSERVATIONS

ON THE NEW ILLUSTRATIONS,

BY

MR. JAMES STEWART,

THE ARTIST WHO MADE THE DRAWINGS.

THE ENTELLUS MONKEY.

PLATE IX.

From a Specimen in the Edinburgh Royal Zoological Gardens.

THIS rare Monkey, of which there have been several specimens in these Gardens, thrives very ill in this climate, never showing any activity, being always dull and heavy, although never fretful; showing very little agility or disposition to playfulness, even though surrounded by others, sporting all manner of antics. It sits amidst the bustle with dull glaring eyes, totally indifferent to every effort made to induce it to join the fun along with the rest. The specimens at the Gardens have varied in colour, from a dull fawn all over the body, lighter beneath, to a pale ashy white; face in all the specimens purplish-black; hands of a dead flesh colour.

CERCOPITHECUS MONA.
THE VARIED MONKEY.

PLATE X.

*From a Specimen in the Edinburgh Royal Zoological
Gardens.*

THIS portrait was taken from one of a pair at present in the Gardens. It is one of the most active, pleasing, and beautiful of all the Monkey tribes; keeping its naturally fine coloured and textured fur scrupulously clean. It is extremely good natured, active, and graceful, in all its movements; very inquisitive; fond of handling and examining every object within its reach; yet, with all its apparent familiarity, never permitting itself to be handled. It will at once put out its hands, and examine the back of your hand, lift the cuff of your coat, examine your wrist-band, scrutinizing every part with magpie and marrow-bone like expression; but, upon the slightest symptom of turning up the palm of your hand, it withdraws its hands with the speed of thought. When given any thing to eat, even its most common food, it applies it with both hands to its nose, then deliberately examines it, applies it to the nose again, and, convinced of its quality, it begins carefully to remove any skin, husk, or blemish; after which it eats quickly, but not greedily. When, after such examination, it is not satisfied with any thing offered, it lets it drop from its hands, looking after it in its descent, uttering a low guttural sound, the only sound it utters except a squalling scream when excited.

CERCOCEBUS FULIGINOSUS.
THE MANGABEY OR WHITE EYELID MONKEY.

PLATE XII.

From a Specimen in the Royal Zoological Gardens, Edinburgh.

THIS Monkey is good-natured and playful, yet, in its most humorous fits, displaying a ludicrous gravity of expression, at the same time uttering a low, pleased, serious grunt. It was exceedingly inquisitive, fond of handling and examining every thing within reach, yet carefully keeping itself clear of being touched; never showed any fits of passion or ill-nature; was not greedy or grasping; took what it got from visitors in the way of dainties, never appearing jealous of much smaller or weaker companions in the same cage, who came in for a share of the good things going. It walked mostly

on all fours; sometimes carried its tail erect, but
for the most part elevated about and horizontal
with the back. The back remarkably straight and
stiff, appearing not to have the same flexibility of
spine, possessed by Monkeys in general.

CERCOCEBUS SABÆUS.
THE GREEN MONKEY.

PLATE XIII.

*From a fine Specimen (out of three or four) in the
Edinburgh Zoological Gardens.*

THIS is an exceedingly active, cleanly, and graceful
Monkey, familiar and confident, yet not obtrusive
or quarrelsome; but, if roused, attacking boldly, and
intimidating much larger and stronger Monkeys
than itself. When offered a nut, it did not, like
many of its companions, snatch it from the hand;
but took it slowly and confidently. It would then
roll it between the palms of its hands; then wet it
in its mouth, rubbing it repeatedly on its hip, till
apparently satisfied that it was clean enough; it
would then crack it and eat the kernel.

This Monkey appears not to thrive well in confinement, as several fine specimens, which have
been in the Gardens, lived but a very short time.

MACACUS SILENUS.
THE WANDEROO MONKEY.

PLATE XIV.

From a Specimen in the Edinburgh Zoological Gardens.

THIS is a very beautiful, gentle, and familiar little Monkey, exceedingly active, and in all its motions, displaying a quiet intelligence; at the same time, looking you in the face with a pleased and peering human-like expression; fond of handling and examining every thing; at the same time allowing itself, without the least shyness, to be fondled, expressing its satisfaction by a laughing look; showing its teeth, and applying them gently to the hand, licking it, &c. It shows no selfishness; but holding out its little hand with a grateful look, will take any of the good things offered, of which the younger visitors are seldom forgetful. It does not show the least anger, although its smaller companions should snatch from its hand the bite going into its mouth.

The only sound it emits, is a low pleased nicher: and, when excited, a clear sharp whine.

ATELES PANISCUS.
THE COAITA.

PLATE XX.

From a Specimens in the Edinburgh Royal Zoological
Gardens.

THERE have been several specimens of this Monkey
in the Gardens, from time to time, all possessed of
the same characteristics—extreme gentleness and
timidity. Suffering much from cold when in the
shade, in our warmest summer weather; its most
common posture, when at rest, was sitting, its head
resting between its knees, its long arms being
folded round them, and clasped on its back, its
long tail twined round, and twice encircling its
lower extremities. In this position it would sit for
hours, marking, with the keenest attention, every
thing occurring within range of its sight. When
offered any thing tempting to eat by any of the
visitors, it would slowly unfold itself, as if fearful to

expose itself to cold; and, with pursed mouth and protruding lips, uttering a plaintive and fretful gutteral whine; would slowly and deliberately take hold of any thing given to it, by a sidelong movement of its long narrow hand, divested of even the rudiments of a thumb; and placing the hollow of its closed hand to its mouth, would pick out any thing it contained. Its gait and movements about its cage were agile, but cautious, never making a leap from one part to another, but climbing quickly about, holding on and letting go with hands, feet, and tail alternately. It was very fond of thrusting its long cold hands between the palms of yours, being pleased with the warmth that yours imparted; always uttering its usual whine when you shook yourself clear of it. The smallest Monkey in the same cage tyrannized over it with the utmost impunity. When irritated, which seldom happened, it uttered a short barking grunt.

CEBUS MONACHUS.
THE LARGE HEADED SAPAJOU.

PLATE XXII.

*From a Specimen lately in the Royal Edinburgh
Zoological Gardens.*

THERE was a fine specimen of this Monkey in the
Gardens about two years ago; it was exceedingly
timid and morose, yet not ill-natured or mischievous, always keeping as far away from the
visitors as it could, by clinging to the higher bars
of the cage; avoiding, with equal care, its fellow
inmates; by whom, although much smaller and
weaker, it underwent a constant system of perse-
cution. By the way of bettering its condition, it
was removed into a cage, containing four or five
Racoons; but they turned out to be of "the wicked
whose tender mercies are cruel;" as they one night,
by way of a ploy, took the liberty of killing and
eating him.

CALLITHRIX SCIUREUS
THE SIAMIRI.

PLATE XXIII.

From a fine Specimen in the Zoological Gardens.

THIS animal lived but a short time in the Gardens.
Unfortunately, it arrived in this country near the
fall of the year, and the coldness of the climate soon
put an end to its existence.

In its habits it was quiet and gentle, never showing the least symptom of petulance or ill-nature in
its movements. On all-fours it was quick but deli-
liberate, never springing nor jumping; but, with a
quick running movement, which it generally made
in pursuit of flies, of which it seemed very fond,
always catching them by a movement of the hand,
so quick as to be imperceptible. Before eating its
prey, it carefully removed the wings, and if a small
fly, it eat it entire; if a carrion or blue-bottle fly,

of which there are great numbers about the Gardens, it would divide the fly, eating only one-half at a time.

If offered any thing eatable, it held out its hand with extreme caution, fixing its large eyes on yours. If the least motion of the other hand were made, it excited suspicion, and it would immediately withdraw to the middle of the cage, the place farthest removed from danger, uttering a low chittering sound, and hardly any inducement would tempt it from its security again. In walking, its back was much arched, shoulders very low, head higher than the shoulder, tail always drooping.

OUSTITI.—THE STRIATED MONKEY.

Plate XXVII.

From a Specimen in the Edinburgh Royal Zoological Gardens.

There have been numerous specimens of this beautiful yet extremely delicate little Monkey in the Gardens, whose short stay there was a mere process of suffering and decay, as they appear to pine from their first arrival. There whole care, when not eating, appeared to be huddling together to protect themselves from cold, almost constantly uttering their low plaintive chitter; a shivering motion being always perceptible throughout their attenuated and crouched-up frames. The only object that seemed for a moment to rouse their dormant and feeble energies, was the occasional intrusion of an unlucky fly into their cage, which was instantly seized, divested of its wings, divided in two, and greedily devoured. Indeed, from the avidity with which they hunted these insects, and the relish with which they ate them, they appear to be, in a great part, their natural food.

CPSIA information can be obtained at www.ICGtesting.com

264962BV00007B/55/P

9 781164 187622